DEDICATION

This book is dedicated to my father, Michael T. McGovern, who was always my biggest fan. In life he taught me to smile in the face of adversity; his sudden death in 1986 taught me to live life to the fullest.

ACKNOWLEDGMENTS

I'd like to use this small space to thank all those who have helped to keep me happy and healthy as I've pursued my dreams: my mother Judith, sister Jennifer, brothers Michael and John, and Aunt Pat, for their support and encouragement; my "World Class" sponsors: New Balance, Polar Heart Rate Monitors, and PowerBar for helping to pay the bills; The University of Rochester, The West Indies Laboratory for Marine Sciences, The University of Wisconsin-Parkside, The University of Maryland, The University of Virginia and LaGrange College for rolling over my student loans and keeping me happily out of the job market for half my life; Mark, Linda and Seth at Walking Magazine for deeming my stuff worthy of publication; my fellow National Team members for keeping it fun; and my long-suffering girlfriend, Mo, who's nice to me even if I am a guy.

Good coaches and self-coached athletes need to be great plagiarizers: I'd like to thank the great coaches and athletes of the world who've given me ideas and guidance, answered burning questions and helped me to sort things out over the course of my athletic career and my development as a coach: Frank Alongi, Owen Anderson, Simon Baker, Roy Benson, Martín Bermudez, Tim Berrett, Bohdan Bulekowski, Sal Corrallo, Mike Dewitt, Dr. Sergio Granados Diaz, Boris Drazdov, Mark Fenton, Jerzy and Andres Hausleber, Craig Hilliard, Howard Jacobson, Leonard Jansen, Bill Markiewicz, Dr. Hector Aguilar Mendoza, Carlos Mercenario, Billy Mills, Magnus Morenius, Les "Leicester" Morton, Howard Null, Jan Olsson, Howard Palamarchuck, Tom Perrin, Mike Rohl, Martin Rudow, Jeff Salvage, Carl Schueler, "Coach Sha," Harry Summers, Rich Torrellas, Gary Westerfield, Ian Whatley, Zhao Yongshen, Dave Yukelson, and Li Zewen.

Many thanks to Gary and Howard Null for making the Healing Springs Racewalking camps such a huge success, and to Tom Eastler for doing the same for the University of Maine Camps. Thanks also to all those who have opened their homes and done the leg work to host my Dave's World Class clinics.

Finally, much gratitude to Monetta Roberts, Bob Bowman, and Debby Van Orden for editing the final manuscript, to Frank deGruy for helping with the layout and graphics, and to Tom McQuade, who's never been thanked by anyone for anything:

THANK YOU!

FOREWORD

If you could have one of the following as your personal walking coach, who would you choose?

1. An entertaining, engaging coach who has given literally scores of intensive weekend and week-long clinics throughout the country for walkers of all stripes, from aspiring junior athletes to fitness enthusiasts to fiercely competitive masters racewalkers.

2. An athlete who has been on numerous U.S. racewalking teams, has attended many U.S. national team and international training camps, and who has traveled the world for competition.

3. A 35-year-old itinerant racewalker with a master's degree in environmental planning and a penchant for wearing Mickey Mouse sunglasses in races and tossing his cookies with disturbing frequency (and force) in hot-weather competitions.

Certainly number one, you say, and perhaps number two, because of his competitive experience. And the great news is that this book is the accumulated wisdom of a man who is a hybrid of exactly those credentials.

The secret, however (though no longer closely guarded) is that the author is also number three–a yet to be full-time employed, fun-loving, less than conventional competitor who, when he races well, can race very well (apparently the glasses work), but who can also crash and burn spectacularly (apparently the mid-race hurling does not).

Interestingly enough, it may well be this third element–a disdain for convention, and more than a fair share of adversity in his competitive career–that make this book such an entertaining, readable and valuable resource.

I've known Dave since 1984, during his days as an undergraduate at the University of Rochester, and over years of training and competing with him, and later running some of the U.S. National Team training camps he attended, I found him a true student of the sport. I also found him to be a lot of fun to be around. A tough competitor who always looked for the next training breakthrough or nutritional tip to gain an edge, he was willing to try it all: punishing anaerobic threshold workouts, VO2 max intervals, even my pre-race strawberry frosted PopTart ritual (although the latter seemed better suited to my 50km distance than to Dave's speedy 20km sprints which, research found, required the more conventional cheeseburgers and fries approach).

As such, Dave's laboratory has been his own body, and in reading and chuckling your way through this book you'll be the beneficiary of all those experiments; both the successes and the failures like the one that ended in dehydrated, disoriented "Swailing" at the 1995 World Cup in Beijing, China.

You'll enjoy the passion and energy that Dave puts into all his endeavors, from his World Class clinics and his goal of visiting every one of America's National Parks (46 out of 53, so far, and counting...), to researching and writing articles for *Walking Magazine.* The result is an informative, yet far from ponderous, collection of science and personal wisdom certain to have you at least laughing, if not walking faster, in no time.

Mark Fenton
Editor at Large,
Walking Magazine

PREFACE

I started this racewalking thing as a joke back in 1982. I was a decent cross-country runner and a miler on my high school track team, but I spent more time cutting through the neighbors' yards to jump into their swimming pools than actually training. Back in the 1970s and early 1980s there were 1-mile racewalks in all New York State high school meets, from dual meets all the way to the state championship. One day I had a bad race at the mile, so I jumped into the walk to get a workout— and to goof on my friend Joe Cambria, the "real" walker on the team. I took third in the race, right behind Joe, but we both had our points taken away because I hadn't actually signed up to do the event. We wound up losing the meet, so our coach made me walk the rest of the season as punishment.

The next season my coach convinced me to continue walking. He wanted the points, but since he didn't know anything about racewalk training he gave me free rein to coach myself and the three girls who racewalked for the team. I liked my new role as "Coach Dave" and did as much as possible to learn about the event to help myself and the athletes I was now coaching. I read everything I could find, but the information back then—as now—was pretty scarce. We did okay, but the few articles I did find weren't a very good substitute for good coaching.

The following September I happily began a new life as a retired racewalker at the University of Rochester. But before long, the assistant track coach—a racewalker himself—found out that I had once been a walker and blabbed his discovery to Andy Liles, the 1983 Junior National Racewalk Champion and a fellow U of R student. Hoping to recruit a new training partner, Andy convinced me to start training again to prepare for the 1984 Junior Nationals. That lasted until February, when I slipped on a patch of ice while training and broke my leg. Andy retired when he lost me as a training partner, but after six weeks in a cast I began walking again to rehabilitate the leg. I trained hard for the Junior meet, which was being held in conjunction with the '84 Olympic Trials, and won a controversial silver medal. Controversial, in part, because I finished the 10K race in 2nd place, but the lap counters made us walk an extra lap. Coming around the last turn of the 26th lap I began vomiting just as I was being passed on the inside by Eric Schmook. One of the referees saw me heaving just as Eric brushed by me. Although it was the barfing that caused me to stumble into lane three, Eric was ultimately disqualified for the contact.

I wound up earning a free trip to the Pan American Juniors meet in the Bahamas where I took the bronze medal behind my good friend, Carlos Mercenario. Carlos went on to win three World Cup titles and an Olympic silver medal, and I went on to do whatever it is that I've been doing for all these years. And Eric? Well, he quit walking pretty soon after that. If it weren't for that little barfing problem that still plagues me in most of my longer races, I would have missed out on the Bahamas trip and probably wouldn't be walking, coaching or writing this book today. Fate's a funny thing....

What started as a joke has become my passion. I've traveled all over the world to compete and to learn how to improve my own racewalk technique and training. I found that other athletes and coaches were perfectly willing to share their ideas with me, but it struck me that none of this valuable information was being passed down beyond the elite level. So in 1991 I decided to do something about it.

While training at Healing Springs Ranch, a health spa in rural Tioga, TX—birthplace of Gene Autry and home of world-famous Clark's Barbecue—I decided to host a series of racewalk training camps. My idea was to invite top coaches and U.S. National Racewalk Team members to Tioga to pass on some of their combined knowledge to masters walkers who were willing to spend a week at The Ranch to learn from the best. And they were the best: Coaches Bohdan Bulekowski, Mark Fenton and Ian Whatley; sports psychologist Howard Null; National Team members Mark Bagan, Andrzej Chylinski, Curtis Fisher, Jonathan Matthews, Herm Nelson and Dana Yarborough all made the trip to Tioga to lend a hand.

The camps were a huge success, but it bothered me that between the cost of flying to Texas, and room and board at The Ranch, a trip to Tioga was too expensive for all but the most dedicated walkers. So I decided to take the show on the road: Instead of having 20 people fly to Texas for a camp, I decided to fly to them. My World Class weekend clinics have afforded me the opportunity to reach far more people than I could ever have hoped to reach in Tioga.

But there was still a problem. Having all this great technique and training information at my disposal has helped my own walking tremendously. Now I'm in my 30s, but I'm walking times I couldn't have imagined even five years ago. So, with my own training and competition schedule to contend with, I only have about 15-18 free weekends per year to conduct clinics. Hence, the book.

The Complete Guide to Racewalk Technique and Training distills 20 years of accumulated racewalking knowledge into a single source—a complete reference for anyone wanting to walk faster and more legally. Although this book is no substitute for good one-on-one coaching, the easy-to-understand technique tips and common-sense approach to training are a great resource for the coached and self-coached racewalker alike.

CONTENTS

SECTION I: TECHNIQUE

SECTION II: TRAINING

SECTION III: PSYCHOLOGY

SECTION IV: IT AIN'T JUST WALKIN'

SECTION V: COMPETITION

SECTION VI: LOOSE ENDS

SECTION I: TECHNIQUE

LEARNING TO FLY WITH ONE FOOT ON THE GROUND

Although walkers are guided by the same general principals as other endurance athletes, racewalking is a unique discipline within track and field. Elite 10km and 20km racewalkers must maintain stride frequencies comparable to those of Olympic 1,500-meter runners, yet they have to sustain these turnover rates for between 42 and 90 minutes, compared to 3 1/2 minutes for the runners. To achieve such stride frequencies, racewalkers must train as much for technical proficiency as for physiological or psychological superiority—failure to train all these areas will leave the walker less than completely prepared for the rigors of competition. This book—the kind of resource I wasn't able to find in my early days as a coach and athlete—will give budding racewalkers a strong foundation on which to build their future training in all these areas, beginning here with technique training.

Chapter 1: A Brief History of Racewalking

The sport of racewalking and the fast, fluid technique practiced by today's elite racewalkers has witnessed almost continuous change over the centuries as it has evolved into its present incarnation. Modern racewalking can trace its roots at least as far back as late 16th century England, as noblemen bet large sums on match races arranged between their footmen. At that time no serious attempt was made to codify the rules by which these competing servants progressed—the only condition was that "fair heel and toe" be practiced. Occasional "trotting" was even permitted as necessary to ward off cramps. These private match races in time evolved into public foot races where "betting reached such a height that spectators stood along the highway eagerly placing their wagers as the contestants passed."

"Fair heel and toe" continued to define walking until the end of the 19th century as racewalking developed into a *bona fide* amateur track and field event in Britain. A seven-mile walk was included on the program of the first-ever Amateur Athletic Club of England Championships in 1866, and one or more walking races at distances between two and seven miles have been included in every edition of the championships since. Before the turn of the century the British Race Walking Association led the way in defining rules for the growing sport. The "model walker" was described as having "...a long stride, straight knee, toes well up, complete hip action, upright carriage, [and a] vigorous arm swing."

Due to the sport's popularity in Britain and the United States around the turn of the century, an 880-yard racewalk was included on the Olympic program at the 1904 Games in St. Louis as part of the "all-rounder" competition—a ten-event precursor to the decathlon. Continued interest in walking was such that 1,500- and 3,000-meter racewalks were contested at the 1906 "Interim" Olympic Games at Athens, and 3,500-meter and 10-mile races were held at the 1908 Games in London. Since that time, one or more racewalks have been included in all but one edition of the Olympic Games.

These early Olympic walks continued to be judged on the basis of unwritten principles of "fair heel-and-toe," with judges forming their own opinions concerning a walker's legality—if it looked like walking it was legal. Beyond these subjective, aesthetically based judgments, there were still no concrete written rules to define legal racewalk technique.

It should come as no surprise then, that judging controversies plagued these early racewalks. Disqualifications in the 1,500- and 3,000-meter racewalks at the 1906 Games, and the 3,500-meter and 10-mile walks in 1908 led to a number of protests by the affected athletes. Conditions deteriorated at Stockholm in 1912 as six entrants were disqualified, leaving only four finishers in the 10,000-meter event.

Because of these and other controversies, an international governing body was created to oversee athletics, as track and field and its related disciplines are known outside the United States. The International Amateur Athletic Federation (IAAF) was created in 1912 to govern track and field, long distance running, cross-country running, and racewalking.

Despite the placement of IAAF-certified judges, controversy once again erupted over the walks at Antwerp in 1920. A number of walkers in the field were disqualified, leading to the strongest showing by American walkers ever. U.S. athletes finished 3rd, 5th and 8th in the 3,000 meters, and 2nd and 6th in the 10,000 meters.

Beaten by the Americans, and fearing removal of the troublesome walks from the Olympics, the British responded in 1922 by drafting the first rules to govern racewalking. The British Road Walking Association provided this first formal definition: "Walking is a progression by steps so taken that the heel of the foremost foot must reach the ground before the toe of the other foot leaves it."

Despite the new definition, controversies continued to dog the walks. At the 1924 Games in Paris, an Austrian was disqualified in an early heat of the 10,000-meter walk but was permitted to enter the finals after a jury of appeals overruled the racewalk judges. Upset by the reversal, the judges resigned and a new panel had to be found before the event could continue.

After the Paris debacle, the walks were left off the program of the 1928 Olympics in Amsterdam. Following the Games, the IAAF met in Amsterdam to establish an improved set of rules for competitive racewalking and the judging of the sport. The wording of the definition of racewalking was simplified to: "Walking is a progression of steps so taken that unbroken contact with the ground is maintained." The Amsterdam conclave also eliminated the difficult-to-judge shorter track races. The racewalk became a long-distance endurance event, reappearing at the 1932 Games at Los Angeles as a 50km road walk.

After World War II, the British lobbied the IAAF and the International Olympic Committee (IOC) for an Olympic track walk to provide exposure for the racewalking. A 10km walk was reinstated at the 1948 Games in London as well as at the 1952 Games in Helsinki. The distance was then increased to 20 kilometers for the next Olympic Games, in Melbourne in 1956. The 20km and 50km racewalks have become the standard IAAF distances for men; both events have been included in every Olympic Games since 1956, with the exception of the 1976 Games at Montreal where the 50km was dropped as a consequence of "down-sizing" the Games. 20km and 50km walks are also contested at the IAAF Track and Field Championships, the IAAF World Race Walking Cup, and regional competitions like the Pan American Games, the Commonwealth Games and the Asian Games. There is also a 20km walk at the Goodwill Games.

Women's walking began in earnest at the world level only in 1968, with the inception of an annual 5km "World Meeting." But women's walking caught on rapidly; so much so that in 1979 the first "Eschborn Cup" was held in conjunction with the men's Lugano Cup finals in Eschborn, West Germany. Now a women's 20km race is held as part of the biennial IAAF World Racewalking Cup on equal footing with the men's 20km and 50km races. With the addition of a women's 10km racewalk to the Olympic program in 1992, and the doubling of that distance to 20km beginning with the 2000 Games, women are now finally able to share the same competitive opportunities that men have enjoyed since the turn of the century. In addition to the Olympics and the IAAF World Race Walking Cup, Women's National Team members now compete with the best female walkers in the world at the IAAF World Track & Field Championships, the Goodwill Games, the Pan American Games, the World University Games, and a number of other international competitions.

Chapter 2: The Evolution of Racewalking Technique and the Development of the Rules

Clearly, racewalking technique has undergone a marked evolution from its early roots to the remarkably fast, fluid athleticism practiced today. The men's track record for 20km, held by Ecuador's Jefferson Perez, stands at a mind-boggling 1:17:21. That works out to under 6:15 *per mile* for 12.4 miles. Women walk 7:00 per mile for 20km. These walkers are obviously superbly conditioned athletes; but technique is a major part of the equation as well.

Before racewalking rules were codified, athletes pushed their "fair heel-and-toe" ambulation to the edge of the rather arbitrary limits set by the judges. As the rules have developed, athletes have refined their techniques to walk as quickly as possible within the constraints of these rules. In fact, modern racewalk technique and the rules that govern the sport have evolved in response to one another—as the athletes have gotten faster, the rules have been revised to bar "innovations" that would have taken the sport beyond its original concept as race *walking*. The compromise is a system that permits the athletes to compete as "real" athletes, but without gaining unfair advantage. Good technique allows these athletes to walk as fast as their fitness will allow them to without having to slow down for fear of disqualification.

The Rushin' Russians and the Magnificent Mexicans

According to Australian National Racewalk Coach Harry Summers, the 1956 Olympic Games was one of the major milestones in the development of modern walking technique. Soviet coaches, the first to seriously scrutinize the racewalking gait, advised their athletes to start the walking stride by landing with the heel of the lead foot as close to the body as possible. The faster turnover rates generated by the new technique enabled the Soviet athletes to sweep all three medals in the 20km racewalk and to take the silver in the 50km. Some judges had trouble accepting the new "quick-stepping" technique, but the Russians were walking according to the rules as written, so the judges adapted.

The emergence of elite Mexican walkers on the international scene— beginning with José Pedraza's Olympic silver medal in 1968— represented another quantum leap in both racewalking technique and speed. Mexican National Coaches Alfonso Marquéz and Jerzy Hausleber built upon the Soviet studies and the superior flexibility of the Mexican athletes to teach a technique that maximized stride frequency *and* effective stride length behind the body. The result was a continuous string of successes including numerous Olympic and World Championship medals, and a number of world records.

The Champion Chinese

The most recent innovation in modern racewalk technique has come from the Chinese. Since the mid-1980s the Chinese have been rising to the top of the world rankings by carrying the "quick-stepping" technique to its extreme. Whereas the Mexicans have walked with a pronounced front-to-back hip drive, the Chinese have maximized their stride frequency by all but eliminating hip action. The unconventional technique led to DQ problems for several of the Chinese walkers in the 1987 World Cup and other international competitions. But, as in the past, the judges and athletes have reached agreement on the limits of fair, legal technique and the Chinese have enjoyed continued success. The new technique has gained sufficient acceptance for the Chinese walkers to have won all three events at the 1995 World Cup in Beijing.

The Straight-On-Contact Rule

One of the technique innovations that IAAF judges have not permitted is a bent knee on contact. During the 1980s walkers began experimenting with a "soft knee" on contact. This allowed for maximum stride frequency, especially in taller, longer-legged athletes. (Russian authors also suggested the technique was beneficial in relieving shin pain.) But many athletes failed to achieve full straightening as the leg passed through the vertical support phase. The IAAF responded to the problem by requiring a straight leg "from the moment of first contact with the ground until in the vertical position." The rule change has not been without controversy. Some walkers—especially older walkers— who may not have had trouble under the old rules, are now being disqualified in races. This is certainly unfortunate, but I truly believe that the new rule renews the integrity of the sport. Bent-knee-on-contact racewalking has never looked right to me, and I've always taught my walkers to use a straight-on-contact landing. I believe it's more efficient, as well as better looking. The next chapter will further discuss the rules currently governing the sport.

Chapter 3: More on the Rules

Section V of the USATF Rule Book deals with racewalking. The rules, as amended in January 1996, are as follows:

DEFINITION OF RACEWALKING

Race Walking is a progression of steps so taken that the walker makes contact with the ground so that no visible (to the human eye) loss of contact occurs. The advancing leg must be straightened (i.e., not bent at the knee) from the moment of first contact with the ground until in the vertical position. Disqualification for failure to adhere to the above definition is governed by Rule 39.

Rule 39 discusses the judging of race walking. From rule 39:

JUDGING

1.) The Judges of Race Walking shall have the sole authority to determine the fairness or unfairness of walking, and their rulings, thereon shall be final and without appeal. Judging decisions are made as seen by the human eye.

2.) The appointed Judges of Race Walking shall elect a Chief Judge.

3.) The Chief Judge shall assign the Judges to their respective judging areas and explain the judging procedure to be used during the race.

4.) All the Judges shall act in an individual capacity.

5.) The Chief Judge will serve as the Referee and Chief Umpire if none is assigned. The Judges will serve as Umpires if none are assigned.

6.) In road races, depending on the size of the course, there should normally be a minimum of six to a maximum of nine judges including the Chief Judge. In track races, indoors and outdoors, there should normally be five judges including the Chief Judge.

CAUTION

1.) Competitors must be cautioned by any Judge when, by their mode of progression, they are in danger of ceasing to comply with the definition of race walking (see Rule 150); but they are not entitled to a second caution from the same Judge for the same offense. Having cautioned the competitor, the Judge shall record all such cautions on the Judge's tally card. All Judges' tally cards are turned in to the Recorder at the end of the race for posting.

2.) Each Judge shall use a white paddle or disc for signaling cautions during a walking race. Each paddle or disc should have the symbol ~ indicating a "Loss of Contact" on one side and the symbol > indicating "Bent Knee" on the reverse side to show the reason of the caution.

DISQUALIFICATION

1.) Each Judge's proposal for disqualification is called a warning.

2.) Once a judge has decided to propose a disqualification, the Judge shall immediately fill out a red disqualification card which shall be passed to the Recorder as soon as possible. If there is no recorder, the red cards are to go to the Chief Judge. All warnings shall be recorded separately on the Judge's tally card.

3.) When, in the opinion of three Judges, a competitor's mode of progression fails to comply with the definition of race walking (see Rule 150) during any part of the competition, the competitor having received three warnings shall be disqualified and informed of the disqualification by the Chief Judge.

4.) Disqualification may be given immediately after the competitor has finished, if it is impractical to inform the competitor of the disqualification during the race.

5.) The Chief Judge shall use a red paddle or disc for signaling disqualification during a walking race.

6.) For championship and international trials races, a warning posting *board should be used to keep competitors informed about the number of warnings that been turned in to the Recorder or Chief Judge for each competitor.*

7.) A copy of the completed Judges' Summary Sheet shall be posted as soon after the event as possible.

Sounds awfully complicated, doesn't it? Why do we bother? Because the rules ensure fair competition while allowing the athletes to push themselves to their physical limits. Nobody likes to get beaten by a "cheater;" the new rules make it easier to distinguish pure racewalking from other, less than legitimate modes of progression. Racewalking is *not* simply fast walking—but it isn't "straight-legged running" either. The new rules take some of the blur out of the distinction between these very different activities.

Terminology

As stated in the IAAF rule book, when a walker fails to maintain continuous contact with the ground the infraction is called "loss of contact," or more commonly, "lifting." If a walker doesn't straighten the knees properly he's charged with a "bent knee" or "creeping" violation.

If any of the six to nine judges on the course believe you're in danger of violating one of the rules, they'll usually show you a paddle with a ~ sign for lifting or a > sign for creeping—although they are not *required* to do so. This is called a "caution." Each judge can give you only one caution for each violation per race.

Cautions don't count against you; they can be seen as friendly advice from the judge that you're borderline but not yet walking illegally. If, however, a judge feels that you're definitely violating the rules he'll give you a "warning" or "red card," either with or without first giving you a caution. If you receive three warnings from any combination of judges, you'll be asked to withdraw from the race by the chief judge. This is called a "disqualification," a "DQ" or a "Dairy Queen." Learn these terms—throwing them about fluently will make you very popular at racewalking cocktail parties.

Different Strokes

Whenever I walk in road races, one or more of the runners I beat will ask me, "What's the point? Don't you ever just want to break into a run?

It's faster...." to which I'll respond, "Don't you ever just want to break into a car and drive? It's faster...." Nobody ever said racewalking was the fastest way to get from point A to point B. But neither is running. Swimming the butterfly is not the fastest way to get across a pool, but nobody asks Janet Evans why she doesn't just break into the crawl when she's doing the butterfly or the breast stroke—they're different but equally valid swimming events governed and judged by different rules. Racewalking is a different and equally valid track and field event governed by different rules from the open running events. Just as in swimming, in track and field there are different strokes for different folks.

Just for kicks, next time you're at a track meet ask the hurdlers why they don't just go *around* the barriers or the discus throwers why they don't throw a Frisbee. (After all, it'll go a lot farther....) Why do people think we're so odd?

Are We "Cheaters?"

Outsiders' perceptions of what racewalking is have a lot to do with the ongoing judging controversies that plague our event. It's downright easy for someone with a camera to "catch" a racewalker off the ground for 20 milliseconds (thousandths of a second) per stride—probably about as easy as it is to "catch" a basketball player traveling, or a butterfly stroker doing whatever the heck it is that a butterflyer isn't supposed to be doing. But the rules don't say we can't be off the ground for a very short period of time, they say we can't be off the ground an *excessive* amount of time—excessive meaning longer than that which can be detected by the human eye.

The media love to show photographs of racewalkers off the ground—"cheating," according to the press. The ironic thing is that lifting is not necessarily beneficial to the walker. A bit of simple high school physics, if I may: A body can only accelerate while there is a positive force acting upon it. Once you leave contact with the ground, gravity is the only force acting on you, so you begin to *decelerate*—you begin to slow down.

Having a strong, propulsive push from behind with the rear foot is great, but the longer it takes the front heel to make contact with the ground after the rear foot leaves the ground, the longer it will take before the next propulsive push. So that "flight phase"—the time when both feet are off the ground—does nothing to help you. Lifting, then, is actually inefficient racewalking. So to call a lifting racewalker a cheater is a bit like calling a runner dragging an "illegal" sand bag behind him a cheater.

Finally, to "cheat" at something, you need to be aware that you're doing it. But a very short "flight phase," or loss of contact, is impossible for a racewalker to feel. The walker can only begin to feel flight phase if it lasts more than about 40 milliseconds, which is, conveniently, about the threshold beyond which a judge can begin to see it happening with the unaided eye. So if a racewalker is caught on film walking with a very short flight phase, but he can't feel it, the judges can't see it, and he's not benefiting from it, is it really "cheating?"

Changes in the Wind?

Despite this logic, the IAAF changed the women's international distance from 10km to 20km in 1999 to try to limit "cheating." They have also considered (but rejected) "shoe alarms," high heels on shoes, and further rule changes. But these knee-jerk reactions all stem from the same ignorance of the rules by the media and other "uneducated" spectators who mock our event as a farce. The athletes themselves realize that some walkers have a momentary "flight phase" during their stride, but very few are overly concerned about it—it's an accepted part of the sport.

Putting our detractors in the media aside, our job as racewalkers is simply to walk as quickly as possible with one foot on the ground at all times (as judged by the unaided eye...), while straightening the leg from the point of heel contact to the vertical support phase. All we have to do now is figure out how to accomplish that. Stick around: The following chapters will show you how to racewalk *really* fast while playing by the rules!

Bob Bowman on:
What Racewalk Judges Look for

Accomplishments/Background: Bob is the United States member and Chairman of the International Amateur Athletic Federation (IAAF) Walking Committee. He is a former national racewalking champion and international competitor, who has been an international walking judge since 1977. Bob was a racewalk judge at the 1988 and 1992 Olympic Games and the walking events referee at the 1984 and 1996 Olympics. He has also judged numerous world championship and world cup racewalking events.

Bob Says: "It is really very simple. There are two basic rules: (1) no visible (to the human eyes) loss of contact; and (2) the advancing leg shall be straightened (i.e., not bent at the knee) from the moment of first contact with the ground until in the vertical upright position. A walking judge's role is to ensure that competitors comply with these two basic rules.

"Each judge watches each competitor, ensuring that he or she is in a position to be satisfied that the competitor is walking fairly. If in the opinion of the judge, based on his or her own observations, any competitor is in danger of violating one or both of the two basic rules, then that judge will caution the competitor. This is done by showing the competitor the white caution paddle with the symbol of the violation, either "loss of contact" or "bent knee." A judge can caution each competitor only once for each violation, i.e., for loss of contact or for not straightening the lead leg from the moment of first contact until in the vertical upright position. The judges are instructed to give the walkers the benefit of the doubt by cautioning them if they are not sure that a clear violation has occurred. However, the walkers should take these cautions seriously. They often indicate that more serious problems with their technique could occur if gone unchecked.

"Should the judge decide that a competitor is definitely not walking according to the rules, the judge will then warn that competitor by recording the violation on a red card which is given to the recorder for posting. Three warnings from three different judges will result in a competitor being disqualified. These three warnings can be for either a violation for loss of contact or bent knee or a combination of both. Any three red card combination of these two types of violations will result in the walker being disqualified. Obviously, if a walker starts to receive warnings (red cards), he or she needs to do whatever they possibly can to correct the situation before it is too late. Sometimes this is difficult to do because of the circumstances (i.e., during a finishing sprint).

"The key danger areas, where a competitor is especially likely to be illegal are:

> (a) during the acceleration at the start,
> (b) while passing another walker,
> (c) during the finishing sprint,
> (d) in the middle of a group,
> (e) while making sharp turns,
> (f) while going uphill and downhill, and
> (g) while taking aid and refreshments.

"Judges are usually watching these areas and situations for any possible violations. Walkers need to be aware of this and concentrate on maintaining sound, legal form during these situations.

"So what should walkers do to ensure good legal race walking form? And what should they do to respond to possible cautions and warnings? First of all, the technique one trains with is usually the technique one uses during races. Therefore, there is no substitute for developing sound legal technique prior to competing in races. Also, sound legal technique is actually the fastest technique! This has often been proven by video studies and analyses of the fastest elite walkers in the world. In other words, maintaining contact and straight leg action results in a faster time. Therefore, walkers need to concentrate on their technique over the entire race distance in order to avoid "floating" or "lifting" as well as bent knees. These faults will result in slower times and cautions and warnings from the judges. So it can easily be said that the judges are actually there to help the walkers with their performances. Judges have no preconceived notions on how many cautions and warnings they will give. They know from experience these calls could vary in number and mix depending on many variables such as the experience level of the walkers, physical condition of the walkers, race conditions and tactics, weather, etc. In one race they may have few calls and another race, quite a few. Walkers need to know this and have confidence in these dedicated officials who are there only to ensure the fairness of the competition.

"If a walker starts to receive cautions during a race, again the walker needs to take this seriously but also remember it doesn't mean the walker is in clear violation of the rules. A single caution in an otherwise clean race is not something to be overly concerned about. However, if a series of cautions is given to a walker, this clearly indicates a dangerous trend has developed. A trend that could easily develop into actual violations and warnings (red cards). If this happens, walkers should respond by concentrating on their form. Relaxing may not be the solution because often loss of contact or lifting, as well as bent knees, is the result of relaxing too much. This is especially the case during the early stages of a race and often when walking in a group. Experienced judges often notice this when observing a pack of walkers. Fatigue can also lead to these violations. It is therefore important that walkers, despite being tired, concentrate on their technique in the finishing stages of the race. Walkers also need to concentrate on their form during all the danger areas previously listed. Why risk a needless warning when rounding a turn or during the start of a race? These are silly and avoidable violations that can be upsetting to the walker during the rest of the race. Using one's head is as important as using one's feet in a walking event!

"I hope these simple yet important guidelines will help the reader in his or her racewalking experiences."

Chapter 4: What Constitutes Fast, Legal Racewalking Technique?

Racewalkers training for gains in fitness must also work towards a technique that will allow them to get through races legally. Nothing can be more frustrating than achieving heightened fitness only to be held back by the judges.

We shouldn't be trying to trick the judges, but technical violations are the reality *at all levels* of competitive racewalking—just as they have been through the entire history of the sport. Walking at high speeds, however, does not necessarily mean walking illegally. According to IAAF Racewalking Chairman and IAAF certified racewalking judge Bob Bowman, "It is exactly the opposite case, with today's elite walkers actually lifting for a smaller length of time than their predecessors years ago, while walking at greater speeds."

Walking legally is the easy part—anyone can walk legally if they go slowly enough. More importantly, we must learn to walk efficiently so that we can move as quickly as humanly possible within the rules of the sport. The rules were intended to slow you down, but with increases in efficiency they don't have to slow you down very much.

Does it sound hopeless? Hardly! With a little patience, you can ingrain technique improvements that will enable you to walk faster— *much faster*—without training any harder. Racewalkers can move *very* quickly with proper technique. But what is "proper" technique?

Keep Out of Your Own Way

Walking speed is a function of your stride length multiplied by your stride rate. To go faster you need to increase one or the other (or both). Since one foot is (theoretically) on the ground at all times, stride length is necessarily limited; to walk faster you must strive to maximize stride rate. Like the sculptor who carves away from the stone anything that doesn't look like some naked goddess holding a pomegranate, you must eliminate anything that isn't directly contributing to fast racewalking. If it's hindering rapid turnover, it has to go. The first thing to remember about fast racewalking, then, is to *keep out of your own way.*

The most common way walkers get in their own way is by *overstriding* (Figure 1A). When fitness walkers or inefficient racewalkers want to speed up, they generally do so not by increasing turnover rate, but by increasing stride length. But trying to increase stride length is counter-productive: The further the heel lands in front of the body at contact, the more force the walker has to generate to lift his body up and over the lead leg. It's a lot like a pole-vaulter planting his pole far forward of his body—he has to run very quickly to get himself up and over the pole. The higher the vaulter holds the end of the pole over his head, the more vertical the pole is when the other end hits the ground, and the easier it will be for him to pivot over the "planted" end of the pole. Similarly, the closer the walker's heel contacts the ground in front of the body, the more vertical the leg will be, and the easier it'll be for him to pivot over the planted heel (Figure 1B). Your legs should not make an isosceles triangle in the double support phase as is seen in fitness walkers and overstriding racewalkers. The legs should be asymmetrical with more leg behind you than in front.

Figure 1.

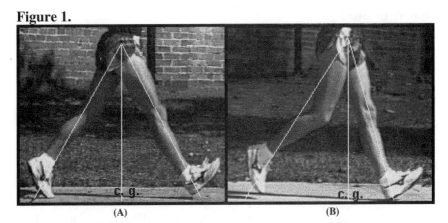

(A)   (B)

Photo (A) shows an inefficient walker's heel landing far forward of a vertical line dropped down from the center of gravity (c.g.); Photo (B) shows the heel landing very close to c.g., and the lead leg almost vertical, making it much easier to "get over" the lead leg. Walker (A) walks inefficiently, with an equal amount of stride in front of and behind c.g. at the moment of heel contact, making an *isosceles* triangle shape with the legs. Walker (B) has about 70% of the stride behind the body, and only 30% in front of c.g. at heel contact, creating a *scalene* triangle. By being asymmetrical, walker (B) does more pushing and less "braking" with each stride than walker (A).

Spin Your Wheels

You may have to sacrifice stride length a bit at first to achieve a high turnover rate—don't worry about it. Efficient racewalking is a lot like "spinning" in a high gear on a bicycle—with a shorter stride it's much easier to achieve a high stride frequency because there's less resistance. In the end, you'll wind up moving forward faster and with less effort. And added speed isn't the only benefit of limiting your stride in front of your body: Those long, slow strides aren't just inefficient, they also *increase* your air time. So shortening your stride length in front isn't just faster, it's actually more legal.

Australian research has shown that in world-class racewalkers heel strike occurs at a point no more than thirty to forty centimeters in front of the center of gravity. And Chinese women—some of the fastest walkers in the world—achieve heel-strike distances of about 10 centimeters. The incredible turnover rates they generate enable them to cover ten kilometers in less than forty-two minutes. Get those heels down quickly and close to the body!

It all sounds great, but how do you learn to take those quick, efficient steps? The whole body is involved, so from the ground up:

Use Your Feet

The feet are the only parts of the body that are ever in contact with the ground while racewalking. An obvious point perhaps, but one that is often overlooked. The feet are a *very* active part of the racewalking motion. But as mentioned above, the first thing to remember is to keep them out of your way. The foot should roll like a wheel or a rocking chair rocker from heel to toe as the body pivots over the lead leg. If the muscles of the foot and the lower leg are weak, the force of the ground acting on the back of the shoe will cause the foot to "flatten out." If the foot flattens out prematurely, the foot will be in the way, hindering forward motion and causing an inefficient, percussive, "stumpy" stride.

Overstriding will cause an even more pronounced flattening, since the heel strikes the ground at a sharper angle. Big, heavy, inflexible, "klunky" shoes will also exacerbate flattening, barring a smooth rolling motion. But more on shoes later.

Keeping your feet out of the way at the front of the stride is critical, but it's equally important to *use* the feet for propulsion and stride lengthening at the back of the stride. Forward propulsion comes from pushing the rear foot *back* against the ground, which creates leverage that will vault you forward. Keeping the rear foot on the ground as long as possible by rolling up onto the toe at push-off will maximize this leverage.

Figure 2.

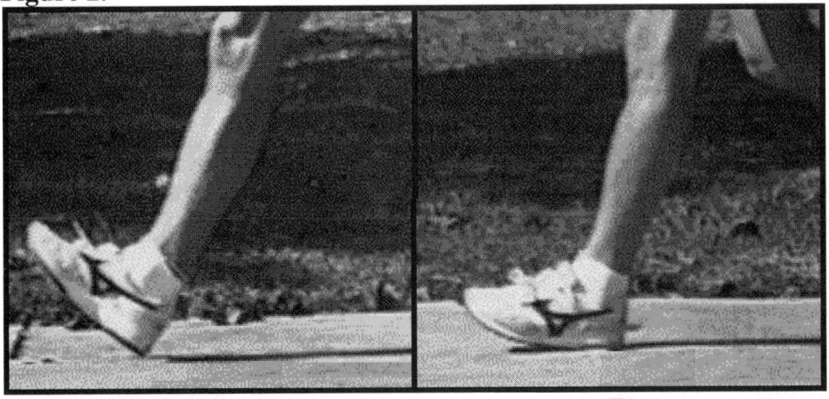

The first sequence shows an overstriding walker whose heel strikes the ground at a very sharp angle (A). The forces acting upon the foot cause it to "flatten out" in front of the body just after heel contact (B), which "puts the brakes on" forward momentum. The second sequence shows a more efficient walker. Since the heel contacts the ground at a much lower angle (C), there is less force tending to "flatten out" the foot, allowing a smooth "rolling" motion to occur (D).

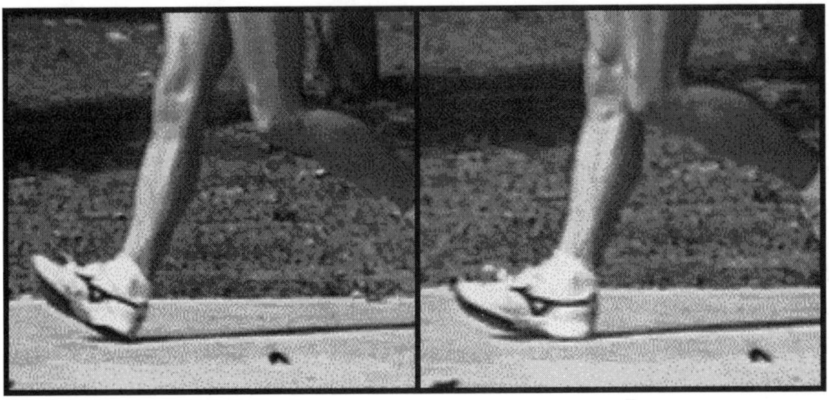

To get the right asymmetrical "look," and to maximize effective stride length and turnover rate, your feet must be very active, rolling smoothly from the heel all the way to the toe with each stride. Failing to do so will result in a "Stumpy" technique and difficulty generating forward propulsion and speed.

19

Weakness and inflexibility hinder effective use of the feet and ankles, but strength and flexibility can be improved. One of the best ways of doing so is by racewalking while wearing a wet vest or other flotation device in a swimming pool. The resistance of the water forces the foot to open and close in relation to the shin. Calf raises and "Theraband" exercises can also be used to strengthen the feet, shins and ankles (see chapter 23).

Toe the Line

Each foot should fall along the same imaginary line as the one before to limit lateral motion of the body and to maximize effective stride length. Proper use of the feet and hips is the key to such "on the line" racewalking. As you push off behind the body with your left foot by rolling up onto the toes, the right side of the hip will swing forward, causing the right foot to land directly in front of the body, rather than out to the side.

Fitness walkers and inefficient racewalkers tend to walk without rolling off the rear foot or using their hips, so the front foot does not land directly in front of the body (Figure 3A). Walking efficiently means using your hips and feet so that the feet fall in-line with each stride as seen in Figure 3B.

Also, if biomechanically possible, the toes should be pointed forward rather than angled out to the sides, to add further inches to your stride. Some athletes walk with the toes pointed out to the sides as much as 30 degrees. Doing so cuts stride length by as much as two inches per stride with no gain in power. Two inches per stride x 200 strides per minute = 400 inches (33 feet, 4 inches) per minute. Over the course of a 10km race that's more than two minutes! Minor technique changes can make a very big difference in race times without requiring that you train any harder.

Figure 3.

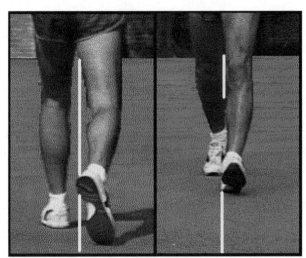

Walker A

Walker B

Walker A walks inefficiently, with the feet landing on either side of an imaginary line. Walker B walks efficiently, using the hips so that one foot falls directly in front of the other along the line, maximizing effective stride length and limiting side-to-side motion of the body's center of gravity.

Use Both the "Driving" and "Vaulting" Phases of Your Stride

Keeping out of your own way is only the first step—now you need to generate some force to propel yourself forward. There are two ways to do this, and you should take advantage of them both. They are the "driving" and "vaulting" components of your stride. The two phases proceed concurrently: As one leg creates momentum by driving forward, the other leg pushes back, launching the body forward by way of a powerful vaulting effect.

Some authors refer to the driving component of your stride as the "swing" phase, but this indicates a passive movement. The knee should drive forward aggressively, as opposed to passively swinging forward. You may also hear the vaulting component of your stride called the "propulsive" phase. This is also a bit of a misnomer, since the legs provide forward propulsion during *both* phases of the stride cycle. Driving and vaulting more accurately describe how the legs generate force throughout the stride cycle.

The driving phase. The driving phase begins with the body in the double-support phase, balanced on the heel of the front foot and the toe of the back foot (Figure 4A). The rear leg then punches forward after the toe of the back foot pushes off the ground. Simple physics: When you take a 25 or 35 pound object—your leg—and throw it forward, the momentum of the moving mass will cause your body to pivot over the planted foot, carrying your body forward. This pivoting is best seen in Figure 4B-D. As the left leg drives forward, the body pivots over the right leg.

Many walkers think the rules say you can't bend your knees when racewalking. Wrong! You can, you should, and you *have to* bend your knees—but only as the leg is moving forward. The advancing leg should drive ahead a lot like a runner's leg, with the knee bending to 90 degrees after push-off, then punching forward vigorously (Figure 4B-C). Think about your arm swing: You bend your elbows at 90 degrees to create a shorter, faster pendulum. You bend your knees to 90 degrees for the same reason: to maximize the speed of the advancing leg.

After punching the knee forward, you use your gluteus and hamstring muscles to pull the leg back; planting the heel on the ground close to the body just as the knee straightens (Figures 4E). Don't try to straighten the knee by contracting the quadriceps muscles: After the thigh changes direction from forward to rearward motion, the momentum of the lower leg continuing to move forward will straighten the knee automatically. Just relax and let it happen. Have you ever opened a swing blade? You flick your wrist, then suddenly stop or change the direction of that flicking motion—the blade opens up as it continues moving in the same direction, straightening just like your leg does at the knee as the thigh changes direction.

One caveat: When driving the knee forward, avoid a high knee lift at all cost. You want your energy going forward towards the finish line, not up. Bringing the knees high is horribly inefficient and it looks illegal as heck. If you punch the knee through low and vigorously, the advancing leg should come through with the foot sweeping very low to the ground (see figure 4B-D). If you get the timing right, your heel should make contact with the ground very close to the body just as the leg becomes straight. It's fast, efficient, and man does it feel cool!

Figure 4.

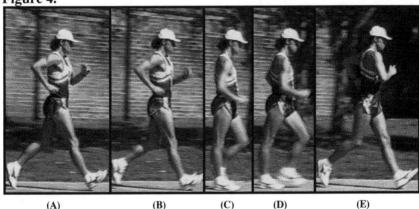

(A)   (B)   (C)   (D)   (E)

This walker demonstrates excellent racewalking technique. The stride sequence begins at the double-support phase (A) with the rear (left) foot pushing off at about a 125-degree angle in relation to the shin. After push-off, the left knee punches forward, bent at a 90-degree angle, initiating the driving phase of the stride (B), with the advancing foot sweeping through very low to the ground (B-D). Notice the support leg (the right leg) beginning to push back, creating a "vaulting" effect (D) concurrent with the "driving" of the left leg. As the thigh of the advancing leg begins to pull back the lower leg swings open and the knee straightens (E). After the left heel contacts the ground, the right knee punches forward to begin the next stride.

Figure 5.

This walker demonstrates poor racewalking technique. The walker leans forward and overstrides, and the feet are inactive.

Figure 6.

A fitness walker, overstriding with bent knees and "dead" feet.

The vaulting phase. The vaulting phase begins as soon as the heel contacts the ground in front of the body. As the bent knee of one leg drives forward, the body passes over the other leg—the straightened "support leg." This is where racewalking differs considerably from running: When a runner's foot is on the ground directly under the body, the knee is bent with the leg "cocked" and ready to *spring* the body forward. Racewalkers, on the other hand, keep the knee straight in the single-support phase, using it as a lever to *vault* the body forward, rather than using a runner's springing action.

24

The key to an effective vaulting phase is to maximize the leverage propelling the body forward. More high school physics: The longer a lever is, the more force it will generate. After the body's center of gravity passes over the planted foot, the calf muscles contract, plantar-flexing the ankle (pointing the toe, as seen in Figure 4A). Rolling off the toe in this manner is one way to lengthen the lever.

Using your hips more effectively is another way to create a longer, more powerful lever. Instead of walking with just your feet and legs, imagine that your leg starts all the way up at the base of your rib cage. Use the hips and the strong oblique muscles along both sides of the abdomen to, in effect, create a longer leg; a longer lever with which to vault yourself forward. Not only will you generate more propulsive force by using your hips, you'll also increase your "effective stride length"— the part of your stride that extends behind your body, pushing you from behind.

Even without actively using your abdominal obliques to create more leverage and open up your stride, a "blocking" effect acting upon the hips will tend to open them up automatically if you roll off the toes properly. As one side of the hip is "anchored" by the leg whose foot is in contact with the ground, the opposite side of the hip swings forward like a gate, carried by the driving knee of the other leg. Proper hip action extends your effective stride length and helps to align the feet "on a line," one in front of the other.

Figure 7.

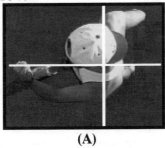
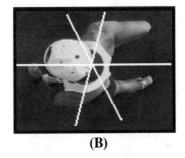

| (A) | (B) |

Walker (A) is not using the hips effectively; overall stride length is limited, effective (behind the body) stride length is relatively short, and the feet are not in line. Walker (B) uses his hips, creating a longer overall stride length, a long stride behind the body, and in-line foot placement.

As you may have inferred by now, our hips are very important in racewalking. Forward propulsion is achieved by pushing the ground behind you with the rear leg, while the advancing leg punches forward with a low, but vigorous knee drive. A strong front-to-back hip action will facilitate both the vaulting and driving phases of the stride. Concentrate on this front and back action rather than the old fashioned side-to-side hip "sashay."

"Hip drop" should occur naturally after push-off: As the rear leg comes forward, and the foot loses contact with the ground, the hip is no longer supported so it drops slightly. This natural effect does not need to be learned, exaggerated, or fretted over—I don't know why so many coaches bother confusing their athletes by talking about it.

Maintain Erect Posture

"Forward Lean" is a myth! Despite being mocked by other coaches and athletes all over the globe, many American coaches still tell their athletes to lean forward five to eight degrees "from the ankles" to try to take advantage of the force of gravity. There are several reasons why this doesn't work: First of all, there's the simple fact that the horizontal acceleration of the advancing leg far exceeds any minor effect of gravitational acceleration. Try standing balanced on one foot, leaning forward five to eight degrees. Now allow yourself to fall forward. You *will* fall forward, but you'll do so by accelerating relatively slowly, then "catching" yourself by extending the other leg out in front of you. It'll take more than one second for your other foot to make contact with the ground; that's three to four times as long as it takes a racewalker walking at 180 to 240 strides per minute to complete each stride. Gravity simply doesn't have enough time to act upon even the slowest moving racewalker to provide any meaningful benefit.

Another major flaw of the "forward lean" technique has to do with that straight leg that catches you as you fall forward. Leaning forward while racewalking artificially forces the lead leg to extend far out in front of the body. This causes a tooth-jarring "braking effect" as you land onto the straight leg like Boris Karloff lurching around the laboratory in his Frankenstein getup. Even if the force of gravity did somehow help to propel Frankenstein's racewalking monster forward—and when I took physics, gravity pulled all the apples, bullets and cannon balls *down,* not *forward!*—the "braking force" of this percussive, stiff-legged landing prevents a smooth transition into the next stride. I could never understand why the villagers always ran away from poor Frank. Sure, a forward leaning, overstriding monster coming after you is scary to look at, but with that inefficient technique, he sure couldn't walk very fast!

So leaning from the waist is ugly and slow, but it's also very hard on the body—on the lower back in particular. Try balancing a broom handle on the palm of your hand. It feels very light when it's standing vertically, doesn't it? Now try holding the broom parallel to the ground by the end of the handle. It feels much heavier. Even holding the broom five to eight degrees beyond vertical is much more difficult than holding it upright. The same thing happens when you try to lean forward when you racewalk. And your torso—supported by your lower back—is a whole lot heavier than any broom handle. I could blather on all day here, but I'll stop now if you promise to straighten up and fly right. Moving right along...

Relax Your Neck and Shoulders

Walking with your head down can cause tension in the neck and shoulders that is transferred to the rest of the body. If possible, focus your eyes on a point on the horizon. If you have to, keep your head level but your eyes down to keep from tripping, kicking road-kill, etc., but do try to look at least 15-20 meters down the road. Wearing a hat with a brim or visor will often cause you to walk with your eyes and head down, so either turn the hat backwards, or simply remind yourself to look ahead while wearing a brimmed hat.

Your shoulders should remain relaxed and as low as possible, and trunk rotation should be minimized. The torso makes up some 40% of the body's mass; any excess upper-body motion will cause substantially increased energy demands and will create tension in the neck and shoulders.

Use a Relaxed, but Effective Arm Stroke

Many "old school" coaches say to "drive with your arms." This is nonsense. Unless you're using ski poles, you do not propel yourself forward with your arms—it's physically impossible! A powerful *rearward* arm stroke does, however, help to initiate a good front-to-back hip action. But keep the arm drive an *effective* arm drive. "Chicken-winging" your elbows out to the sides will cause a side-to-side hip wiggle, while forward "uppercut punches" will alternately raise and drop your center of gravity, adding an inefficient and DQ-drawing "hoppiness" to your stride. Punching the hands too far forward can also cause overstriding to the front of the body, while doing nothing to contribute to forward propulsion.

At worst, your hands should cross in front of the breastbone and swing back vigorously to the hip socket or beyond. Your hands should be relaxed—no clenched fists—and your arms should move freely as if they were pendulums hung from the shoulders. The forearms should be held at about 90 degrees relative to the upper arm, but this will vary depending upon the distance of the race and personal preference. The most important thing is to keep the neck and shoulders relaxed even though the arms are driving back powerfully.

Relax Your Head—Inside

I've said a lot about the action of various body parts, but fast, efficient racewalking doesn't really begin with the feet—it begins with the mind. Relaxation is one of the real keys to walking fast, and relaxed technique begins with mental relaxation. Due to the limitations imposed by the rules, the energy costs of inefficient racewalking accumulate much more quickly than in running. What does that mean? You can fake it to some degree in running, but you'll fatigue and slow down much more quickly when racewalking with inefficient technique.

It's very important to continually remind yourself to relax—especially during stressful races or workouts. You don't need to clench your teeth and fists to walk quickly. Tightness in the jaw and upper body will be referred to the lower extremities, shortening effective stride length considerably. Similarly, attempting to "power" yourself forward by driving with your arms will only result in lifting and costly overstriding. Try not to force things—just relax and let it flow.

An Irrelevant Note On Technique vs. Style

Although used interchangeably by some authors—including me—the terms "technique" and "style" are really not synonymous. Technique refers only to racewalking under the constraints of the rules: Everyone who walks with continuous contact and straightens the supporting leg is exhibiting racewalk technique. Each of these individuals, however, has their own "style." A walker's style is the sum total of all the variations in arm carriage, body posture, hip driv

The rules of the sport make no mention of aesthetics. Many top racewalkers cruise by with an extremely fluid style that may or may not technically allow them to maintain contact with the ground at all times. Other walkers may be less efficient, exhibiting a herky-jerky style that attracts the unwanted attention of the judges. These less efficient athletes may actually be more technically legal than more fluid athletes who often float above the ground for several milliseconds per stride, but the "klunky" walkers are often disqualified by the judges for lifting while the more efficient walkers get by. Is this fair? Maybe not, but it is the reality of the sport. Not only is a smooth walking style faster, more efficient, and less likely to cause injuries, it also gives *the appearance of legality* whether the walker is actually on the ground at all times or not. In the next chapter we'll go over the various ways to learn fast, efficient technique. No wait... I mean style!

And Another Thing...

While we're on the subject of terminological irrelevance, you may have noticed that I refer to racewalk, racewalker, racewalking, etc., as one word. Many dictionaries, spell-check programs and newspaper editors still do not recognize the term racewalk, and refer to us as inconsequential race walkers race walking that goofy race walk thing. Spacewalk has been considered a "real" word for years and we've been doing what we do for a whole lot longer than the astronauts have been doing their thing. The only way to make the change is to use the one-word terms without fail in all publications, and even in personal correspondence. Funk & Wagnalls will eventually get around to recognizing us. Thank you. We now return to our regularly scheduled technique lesson....

Debby Van Orden on:
The Importance of a High Turnover Rate

Accomplishments: 5th Fastest American woman of all-time at 10km (45:07). 4th at the 1992 and 1996 Olympic Trials. 1993 and 1995 World Cup Team member. 1990, '92, '94 and '96 Pan Am Cup team member. 3rd at the 1996 Pan Am Cup.

Personal Record:
10,000 meters: 45:07

Background: Michigan native Debby Van Orden first took an interest in racewalking when she read an article about 4-time Olympic racewalker, Carl Schueler, in *The Wall Street Journal.* Working as a population forecaster in Colorado Springs, CO, Debby realized that Carl worked down the hall from her office at the county government building. She stopped in to meet the "Olympic god" and they became "fast friends." A recreational runner, Debby eventually gravitated towards racewalking, and quickly progressed under Carl's tutelage. Her quick turnover rate as a runner lent itself well to efficient racewalk technique—and at 5'1," Debby needs to maintain a quick turnover rate to walk fast.

Debby Says: "I don't think having shorter legs is a detriment at all. The key to walking fast is not having long strides, but maintaining a high cadence rate. My role model for quick turnover is Annarita Sidoti of Italy, who stands about 4'9" in heels. [Author's note: She's actually 4'11".] She won the women's 10km walk at the '97 World Track and Field Championships, even though she was by far the shortest competitor in the field.

"Even though I have a naturally high turnover rate, I still concentrate on it because it is so important. Once or twice a week I do turnover drills to make sure my stride is always quick and efficient."

Chapter 5: How Do You Learn Fast Racewalking Technique?

The limitations imposed on racewalkers by the contact and straightening rules require that we possess a high degree of neuromuscular coordination to achieve a fast, efficient style. Fortunately, such coordination is trainable if you're willing to put in the time needed to "rewire" your neuromuscular system.

There are three basic ways for a beginning athlete to learn proper racewalking technique, or for an advanced walker to refine the technique that he already possesses: mimicry, modification of a running-based template, and modification of a walking-based template. Which method to use will depend upon the indivdual athlete.

Mimicry

If you've ever racewalked past a herd of adolescents, you've probably noticed them imitating you after you went by. They probably exaggerated the arms and hips a bit, but they usually get it pretty darned close. For some reason, adults tend to over-analyze things instead of "just doing it."

According to former Soviet National Racewalking coach Anatoliy Fruktov, mimicry is by far the most effective way for athletes to learn proper racewalking technique. Fruktov suggests that coaches introduce new athletes to the sport by demonstrating the technique themselves, or by showing slow-motion and actual-speed films of top athletes.

At the same time, the major points of walking mechanics should be explained to the athlete before he is asked to use these elements in practice. Fruktov advises the coach to repeat the demonstration several times at normal speed (170-190 strides per minute) as well as at a deliberately slow pace.

The budding racewalker should then imitate the demonstrated technique at various paces over distances of 50-60 meters. After the athlete tries it a few times the coach should comment on the positives, then point out what still needs further refinement: the ankles, knees, arms, hips or whatever.

The Running Template

If mimicry doesn't work, templates can be used. As stated previously, racewalking is a unique event—it is not fast walking, but it isn't "straight-legged running" either. Despite this basic fact, these two templates can be used in some cases to teach the basic racewalking gait.

Australian national coach Harry Summers suggests using a running template. The athlete is asked to run at about eight minutes per mile for several strides, and then to straighten his legs just before heel contact. In "Placement of the Lead Foot in Racewalking," Summers explains, "it is advisable to use a role model in the teaching of this technique. After observing the action, the walker is asked to jog along at a pace of approximately five minutes a kilometer [8:00 per mile] and gradually change to a straight leg landing. Faults are then corrected. Experience has shown that an explanation alone is not satisfactory, as the action is too fast for the neuro-muscular coordination. Faster results can be obtained with the jogging-straight leg method [than by other means]."

The running template method works best with established, well-coordinated athletes who are attempting to make the transition from running to racewalking. Non-runners with less developed body awareness never seem to get the knee-straightening part figured out when using this method.

The Walking Template

If the walker has trouble with mimicry or the running model, a walking template may be needed. According to former British National walking coach Julian Hopkins, racewalking technique is merely an extension of "ordinary" walking and should be taught as such. To some extent this is the case, but today's walking technique is so far removed from its pedestrian roots that this approach is less effective than the others. Still, a walking template may be of some use to older athletes who are having difficulty learning racewalk technique by other means. Hopkins suggests a four-stage approach to learning the technique. The athlete begins by walking at a brisk but comfortable pace, making certain that continuous contact is maintained, then progresses through the stages by adding on various elements of the racewalking gait: the bent elbows, hip drive, ankle flexion and in-line foot placement.

This method can turn into a laborious process, but it is sometimes effective when other methods fail, and the walker is patient enough to spend the time mastering each step. I use a variation where I concentrate mostly on the feet, having the athletes first walk on their heels with their knees straight for several yards. Then I have them walk on their heels again, this time allowing the toes to drop as the body passes over the foot. Finally, the walkers do more of the same, with extra emphasis on rolling all the way to the tip of the toes as the leg passes behind the body. During the whole process the arms are bent at 90 degrees. If everything works, we usually get a fair approximation of racewalking before too long.

Once the athlete is comfortable with the racewalking technique developed by one of these three approaches, there will most certainly be some flaws to be corrected. At this point a part-by-part approach is needed to iron out these inefficiencies, in which case the demonstrator will explain and show the athlete what still needs more work, be it more hip drive, better toe-off or a more relaxed posture.

Video Analysis

After years of coaching racewalkers I've become pretty good at picking out most technique flaws at a glance. But every once in a while I'll get "stumped." Something won't look quite right in somebody's technique, but no matter how many times they walk by I won't be able to figure out exactly what's causing the problem. But after a few seconds of watching a freeze-frame videotape I'll usually be able to figure it out.

From the athlete's perspective, video affords an opportunity to see the differences between their present technique and that of more advanced or elite walkers, and to get immediate visual feedback after adopting the new techniques. It is an invaluable tool and should be used whenever possible as an adjunct to the three methods described previously. If at all possible, use a quality 4-head VCR or a video camera with freeze-frame and slow-motion capabilities.

Train Your Brain

Anyone who's ever watched a basketball game knows pretty much how to throw a free throw—you stand at the line, hold the ball in one hand, and "push" the ball towards the basket. Same thing with throwing darts: Stand behind the line and toss the thing at the target. Most people even have a pretty good idea how to hit a baseball, juggle live cats or ride a unicycle on a tightrope. Intellectually *knowing how* to do these activities isn't the problem; the trouble lies in actually *doing them*.

Michael Jordan wasn't born with the ability to shoot free throws—and he *definitely* wasn't born with the ability to hit a baseball! He had to miss a lot of baskets (and fastballs) before these actions became reflexive for him.

Once you *cerebrally* learn how to racewalk by working with your coach and seeing yourself on video, you have to repeat the motion many times before it moves back into the cerebellum and becomes part of your *muscle memory*. Dynamic flexibility drills—discussed in chapter 22—will facilitate the process as you repeat specific parts of the racewalking motion. On top of that, it takes a lot of actual time-on-your-feet racewalking to "lock in" efficient, legal racewalk technique. The good news is that once it's etched into your muscle memory, you don't ever have to think about it. By training with good technique every day, you'll "re-wire" your neuromuscular system so that you'll never have to worry about anything during races other than pushing your body to its absolute limit.

Caveats

Although I've said a lot here about refining your racewalking technique, be very careful when making technique changes. All walkers are individuals with unique underlying biomechanical "quirks." Strength, flexibility and morphological imbalances will certainly lead to technique flaws, but it's not always wise to tinker with them. There's probably plenty of room for improvement, but your body will normally tend toward its most efficient state. If you're DQd frequently, injury-prone, or if there's clearly something in your style that's keeping you from fulfilling your potential, it may be worthwhile to make some changes. Just make sure you fully understand the nature of the underlying problem before trying to monkey with your style.

A good coach can help. On the other hand, a well-meaning but inexperienced coach may try to convince you to change something that shouldn't be messed with. In any case, if you do decide that you're in need of a technique tune-up, make one change at a time and phase in any changes slowly to give your body a chance to adapt. Drastic changes to the biomechanics your body has grown accustomed to could lead to injuries—or worse yet: disqualifications!

At the outset it's more important to lock in the new technique than it is to walk fast. Be patient: You may actually have to slow down for a while to give your body a chance to adapt. It's a good idea to avoid races and hard speed workouts for the first four to six weeks after making a change to keep yourself from reverting back to your old habits or getting injured. Once you lock in the new changes, you'll easily be able to get back to—and exceed—your old pre-change training and racing paces.

If you're already a fit athlete, but just learning to racewalk, be especially careful. You'll have the cardiovascular tools to walk fast, but your racewalking-specific muscles, tendons and ligaments will not be fully developed. Avoid the temptation to enter races for at least the first six weeks, or you'll end up like a golf cart fitted out with a rocket engine: It'll go remarkably fast—until the contraption rattles itself apart and winds up in the scrap heap.

Chapter 6: Common Technique Problems and How to Fix Them

The following are a number of common technique problems that I frequently encounter when working with racewalkers at my "World Class" racewalk camps and clinics. These technique problems can lead to disqualification or, worse yet, slowness! The solutions are things I've found to be effective for eliminating these nasty habits.

Problem 1: Flat or slapping feet

Cause: Weak shins, and/or overstriding.

How you know you have it: You hear a loud slapping sound as the foot flattens prematurely in front of your body when you racewalk. Shin pain. "Creeping" calls in races, since the flattened foot causes a lot of force to be transferred to the knee as the body advances over it.

Solution:

Avoid wearing "fat" shoes: Wear "real" racewalking shoes or running flats with a low heel to reduce the amount of leverage acting upon the foot.

- Walk on your heels with straight knees to strengthen the shin muscles, then walk on the outsides of the feet to work the peroneal muscles on the outside of the lower leg. Continue for about 30 seconds, then stretch and repeat several times.

- Perform toe raises for shin strength. Stand with your heels on the edge of a step with the front 3/4 of the foot hanging over the edge. Slowly dip your feet down, then all the way up. Repeat until fatigue forces you to stop—then do five more! Stretch your shins and repeat several times.

- Do elastic band exercises (described in chapter 23) to strengthen your shins.

Problem 2: Overstriding

Cause: Erroneously thinking that long strides must be faster than short ones. Walkers with a fitness walking background often fall into this trap.

How you know you have it: You walk with a very percussive stride. Shin pain. Creeping. Inability to generate speed for even short distances. Lifting and/or bent knee calls in races. People say you're "fitness walking."

Solution:

- Awareness often helps. Simply try to shorten your stride in front of your body when racewalking.

- Perform the "Quick-Step" and "Figure-8" drills (chapter 22) to develop a short, quick turnover.

- Shorten your arm stroke. A short fast arm swing = a short fast leg swing.

Problem 3: "Robot legs"

Cause: Thinking that you aren't allowed to bend your knees when racewalking. Wrong! You can and should bend your knees to about a 90-degree angle as the leg comes forward. It only has to be straight on the way back.

How you know you have it: The advancing leg comes through too straight. People tell you that you look like a robot or tin soldier when you walk. Possibly creeping. You scuff your feet on the ground as they come forward. Also, you're probably slow, and you have no hip drive.

Solution:

- Just do it: Bend the knee more—up to 90 degrees— as the leg advances forward.

- Think about "leading with your knees," driving them low and vigorously with each stride.

- Imagine "punching" a target with your knees. To keep that knee drive very fast and powerful put a face on the target: your mother-in-law, the prom date that stood you up in high school, Katherine Harris— whatever it takes.

- Get to the weight room. Do squats, lunges and other hip flexor-strengthening exercises.

Problem 4: Bent knees ("creeping")

Cause: Various. Overstriding, weak shins, insufficient knee bend during the driving phase.

How you know you have it: Creeping calls and DQs in races. People say you're fitness walking. People mistake you for Groucho Marx. For many people, this is the #1 problem—I put it after overstriding and weak feet and shins in the order here because these are the primary causes of creeping.

Solution:

- Shorten your stride in front of your body. Quickstep drills will help.

- Bend your knees *more* during the driving phase to generate more lower-leg speed. More lower leg speed will help to straighten the knee before the heel makes contact with the ground.

- Walk hill repeats up a gradual incline. Hills force you to take a shorter stride in front, and the extra push from behind needed to overcome gravity helps to straighten the knee.

- Stretch and strengthen the hamstrings, quadriceps and calves.

- Do not use running for cross training.

- Maintain good posture. Bending at the waist shifts the center of gravity forward, over the knee, which may cause it to "collapse" upon heel contact.

Problem 5: "Dead" ankles

Cause: Weak/inflexible ankles and feet. Over-reliance on the driving phase of your stride rather than utilizing both the driving and vaulting phases.

How you know you have it: Your foot makes a 90-degree angle throughout the entire stride cycle—the foot angle never "opens up" in relation to the shin. You have a short stride behind your body. Your head bobs up and down when you walk. Your walking action is not "smooth"—you don't feel like you're "rolling" forward on your foot from heel to toe.

Solution:

- Awareness of the problem often helps. Simply try to roll up onto the toes more at toe-off.

- Racewalk slowly up a gradual incline to strengthen the ankles and calves. Somewhat faster hill repeats may be used to develop an explosive toe-off.

- Perform calf raises. Stand on the edge of a step with the back 3/4 of the foot hanging off the step. Slowly dip the feet down, then all the way up. Repeat until fatigue is felt.

- Use toe-grip exercises to strengthen the bottoms of the feet. Repeatedly pick up a towel or other soft object with your foot by curling your toes around it.

- Perform specific range-of-motion exercises with some form of elastic band or tubing to isolate weak areas of the feet and ankles. Simply loop a heavy elastic band (Theraband, surgical tubing, bungee cord, etc.) around the foot and work the muscles against the resistance provided by the elastic.

Problem 6: No hips

Cause: Tightness, lack of "body awareness."

How you know you have it: People tell you that you don't use your hips. You have a short stride behind your body and a hard, percussive landing upon heel contact.

Solution:

- Stand in place in front of a mirror and practice rotating the hips from front to back in synch with an effective arm stroke.

- Cross your arms over a bit more if you tend to swing them too straight front to back.

- Practice the long-arms drill (Chapter 22).

- Use better foot action, especially a better roll forward onto the toe before push-off. Keeping the rear foot on the ground longer forces the hips to swing open.

- Drive the advancing knee through more powerfully, making sure the knee is bent to 90 degrees. Momentum will help to rotate the hips forward as the leg advances.
- Cross your arms over a bit more if you tend to swing them too straight front to back.

Problem 7: Excessive "forward lean"

Cause: Most walkers who lean forward excessively when walking do so because they've been coached to walk that way.

How you know you have it: Very percussive front foot landing at heel contact ("Frankenstein walk"). People say you lean forward or bend at the waist.

Solution:

- Straighten up! Try to walk in a more upright position. You don't want to lean *back,* but you should definitely ignore any demonic voices in your head telling you to lean forward while walking.
- Pretend someone is pulling you up by your hair while you're walking, or just think about "walking tall."

- Watch other athletes racewalking with a pronounced forward lean. You'll be so horrified you'll never do it again!

Problem 8: High knee lift

Cause: Driving the knees too far up rather than forward. Often seen in former runners, or walkers who have been coached to "prance" like a horse.

How you know you have it: DQs for lifting in races. People say you look "prancy" or "runny."

Solution:

- Forget the horse image.

- Concentrate on driving your knees forward rather than up—aim for a "target" at knee-level.

- Keep your feet very low to the ground as they come forward.

Problem 9: Chicken winging

Cause: Your arms cross your body too much, causing the elbows to poke out to the sides with each arm stroke.

How you know you have it: By looking down at your arms while walking it should be easy to notice that your arm action is more side-to-side than front-to-back. All your competitors have bruised ribs from being banged by your elbows in races.

Solution:

- Practice walking in place in front of a mirror, preferably with small, 3 to 5 lb. hand weights. Watch to see that your elbows remain tucked in. Continue for ten minutes at a time, at least three days per week until the motion becomes very natural.

- Imagine that you're walking in a narrow tunnel. If you don't keep your elbows tucked in they'll bang against the walls.

Final Thoughts

Although every racewalker will develop his or her own individual style, we should all strive to eliminate anything that doesn't move us towards the finish line in a hurry. Imagine carrying a heavy box: Keeping it steady and close to your body is much easier than swinging it to the left and right, or lifting it up and down as you carry it. The same principle applies to your racewalking: If your elbows are chicken-winging out to the sides, if you're toeing in or out, if your hips are sashaying from side to side, or if your center of gravity is bobbing up and down, you're expending a lot of energy in the wrong directions.

Every element of your technique should be compact, efficient, and headed towards the finish line. It may take some time to lock in these changes, but be patient. Once good technique is ingrained, it'll always be there for you when you need it. If you have to slow down a bit at first, by all means, do. It'll pay off in the end with faster times and fewer injuries and DQ calls.

SECTION II: TRAINING

PHYSIOLOGY AND THE LOGIC BEHIND EFFECTIVE RACEWALK TRAINING

Although I figure I've become a pretty good coach by now, I've always thought of myself as more of a teacher than a coach: To do the job properly, a coach really needs to be there every day to get feedback from the athlete. I can coach for a weekend at a clinic, but then I'm gone for months until I'm invited back. I've always felt that *teaching* racewalkers what's going on within their bodies, and showing them how to put together their own schedules is much more valuable than writing out a generic one- or two-month schedule for the group to follow and then leaving town. What happens when the one or two months are up? Repeat the schedule indefinitely? Double everything when you get faster?

If you know what different types of workouts do for you, and you know how to put them together, you can write your own schedules; individual training plans based on how your body responds to training and rest, your individual goals, and your racing schedule. This section will show you how.

Chapter 7: Armchair Physiology

The human body is an amazing machine; a collection of extremely efficient physiological systems capable of doing amazing things—if properly trained to do them. Our ability to adapt to our environment and the stresses we impose upon ourselves in training is the reason that we're able to change ourselves from sedentary couch potatoes to competitive athletes. Knowing a bit about these incredible physiological systems will help.

Gas, Diesel or Propane?

Our bodies are a lot like hybrid cars that can run on a number of different fuel systems. But instead of using solar panels, natural gas and ethanol, we create energy through the aerobic (with oxygen) combustion of fats and carbohydrates when walking slowly, by anaerobic (without oxygen) combustion of carbohydrates when racewalking at a faster pace, and through the direct utilization of adenosine triphosphate and creatine phosphate when sprinting.

Under any conditions we only get about 5% of our energy from protein. The remaining 95% comes from a mix of fats and carbohydrates; the percentage of each determined by the amount of oxygen that we can supply to the muscles, and the muscles' ability to utilize that oxygen.

Like the hybrid car, our bodies tend to utilize the most efficient system available under the prevailing operating conditions. Since some "fuels" are more efficient, more plentiful in the body, or more readily utilized than others, our muscles must "decide" which system to emphasize under different conditions—these conditions mainly being the duration and the pace of the workout or race.

Pros and Cons

Each system has its advantages and flaws: Fat is a great fuel source because it's very energy-dense and it exists in the body in relatively abundant quantities. But since fat can only be burned in the presence of both oxygen and glycogen (intra-muscular carbohydrate), it can only be used effectively as a "low-speed" fuel during easy workouts or long, relatively slow races when there is plenty of oxygen to go around. Carbohydrates on the other hand, are more versatile since they can be burned either with or without oxygen. But since we can only store a limited supply of them in our bodies, carbohydrates can be depleted within as little as 90 minutes of hard work.

Glycolysis, the combustion of carbohydrates for energy, is "bad" for another reason: It's your body's equivalent of a diesel engine—a reliable energy system under a variety of conditions, but when oxygen is limited it's "dirty" as heck. Instead of spewing out smog, however, your anaerobic glycolysis "engine" spits out buckets of nasty lactic acid. The faster you walk, the more lactate you accumulate in your blood and muscles. Lactic acid is a biochemical "bad guy" because it slows down the enzymatic activity within the muscles, preventing them from contracting rapidly; the higher the acid levels, the harder it is for the muscles to contract. Your *lactate threshold* or *anaerobic threshold* is the highest walking intensity at which your body can still produce energy and muscular contractions aerobically, without accumulating fatiguing levels of lactic acid.

It's All About Oxygen

Ultimately, availability of oxygen will dictate how energy is produced, and how "clean" the combustion will be. In any race over 3km, most energy is produced aerobically, so the bulk of your training for these races should be easy, aerobic distance work. Too much speed work, or too many hard miles on the roads will teach the muscles to rely on anaerobic glycolysis, resulting in excess lactate production when racing—not a good scenario.

As walking intensity increases, so does your oxygen intake, or VO_2 (V for Volume, O_2 for oxygen). *VO_2 max* is a measure of the maximum amount of oxygen that your lungs can take in and send to the muscles. After using this oxygen to help burn fats and carbohydrates, carbon dioxide is released as a by-product.

Measuring these gasses is the only *direct* way to determine which systems are producing energy, but the equipment is very bulky so the tests can only be performed by doctors or exercise physiologists in a laboratory setting. That involves getting on a treadmill while you're hooked up to what looks like a cross between a welder's helmet and Mom's old Electrolux vacuum cleaner—not the kind of thing you'd want to wear during your next 5km race.

The Heart of the Matter

Luckily there's an easier way: All that inhaled oxygen has to get to the working muscles somehow, and it does so dissolved in the blood and pumped throughout the body by the heart. As oxygen needs increase, heart rate increases—in lock step with respiration rate. Heart rate, then, is a very reliable—albeit indirect—indicator of oxygen use. That's why the Neanderthals (back in the 60s and 70s) used to stop to take their pulse during workouts. We'll talk more about heart rate later, but for now the important thing to remember is that heart rate can tell you which systems are producing energy at any particular pace.

Your lactate threshold, VO_2 max and your *economy*—the percentage of your VO_2 max that you can maintain during a race without accumulating exhausting amounts of lactic acid—determine, for the most part, how well you can perform in an endurance event like racewalking. Luckily, these variables, as well as overall endurance, can be improved with training.

The Lean, Mean Walkin' Machine

Obviously there's a lot going on "inside" when you train or race. The muscles need to have lots of enzymatically "ready" mitochondria and lots of oxygen to turn food into energy aerobically. If they don't get enough oxygen the muscles will have to produce energy anaerobically and they'll become polluted with contraction-inhibiting lactic acid. So the lungs have to be able to draw in lots of oxygen, the heart has to be able to pump it throughout the body within the blood, and the circulatory system has to have lots of dense capillary beds developed to get that oxygen-rich blood into the working muscles. Finally, the neuro-muscular system must be highly coordinated so that you can walk with fast, economical (oxygen-sparing) technique. All of these systems have to be working efficiently for you to be truly "race ready." The next chapter will discuss different workouts used to train these various systems.

Fat Ain't Just "Dead Weight"

I've heard coaches say that carrying around an extra 10 pounds of body fat is like trying to racewalk while wearing a backpack filled with 10 pounds of fat. Wrong! I'd rather race with that backpack loaded up with *30 pounds* of fat than carry an extra 10 pounds of fat around my midsection. You see, fat is not just dead weight; it's a metabolic leach that siphons away valuable oxygen-rich blood that should be going to your muscles. While muscles "pull their own weight" by using that oxygen to propel you forward, fat stores do nothing to move you towards the finish line—despite being perfused with miles of capillaries.

VO_2 max, which measures your body's ability to take in and use oxygen to create energy, is measured in milliliters of oxygen per kilogram of body mass per minute. Unless you've studied Einstein's *General Theory of Relativity* before lacing up your walking shoes, and you plan on walking near the speed of light, a minute is always going to be 60 seconds. The other two variables—the amount of oxygen you're able to breathe in and your body mass—are subject to change. So to increase your VO_2 max—and greatly improve your race times—you either have to improve your ability to take in oxygen by doing very difficult VO_2 max intervals, or you can decrease your body mass by simply losing a few extra pounds. So what's it gonna be? Lung-searing 800-meter repeats at 95% of maximum heart rate, or a few extra easy miles per day and a slight decrease in your weekly donut intake? It's your decision.

Chapter 8: Types of Workouts

Improved fitness comes from stressing the body, then allowing it to recover from the stress. Known as the General Adaptation Syndrome, or GAS, this principle is the foundation upon which all endurance training is built. You need to work hard a few days per week to stress the body, then take it easy to allow your body to recover fully, adapt, and rebuild itself stronger than it was before the stress of the hard workouts. Any racewalk training schedule must include sufficient and varied hard work to stress all the physiological systems that will be called upon when racing, interspersed with plenty of rest to allow for complete recovery and adaptation.

There are five different types of workouts that you can incorporate into your training, each undertaken at a specific range of speeds or heart rate values, and each affecting different physiological systems. Maximum efficiency in training comes from using these types of workouts and eliminating "junk mileage"—mileage at a pace or heart rate that falls outside the target ranges of these types of workouts. These workouts are:

Rest/Recovery Workouts

Recovery workouts can be either total rest, very easy training, or easy cross-training. Since gains in fitness only occur after *recovery and adaptation* from hard work, these can be viewed as some of the most important workouts of the week. But they can also be the most difficult to do properly. Sometimes it's hard to take an easy day or a day off when you're "on a roll," even if you need it.

Don't get caught up in weekly mileage. If you need to take a day off, don't worry about bringing down your weekly mileage total. Your ultimate goal shouldn't be to see how many kilometers you can rack up each week. Your goal should be improvement as a racewalker, and that's not going to happen if your body can't recover from the hard workouts.

To allow full recovery, you need to walk at a very comfortable pace, but it's important to remember that technique must be maintained at all times—even on easy days. A good rule of thumb is to never train slower than 25% over 5km race pace. Any slower and technique starts to fall apart. Also, don't be afraid to cross-train. Swim, roller blade, go for a long hike. Do something *fun!* If you're too tired to do any kind of workout, get some Ben and Jerry's, flick on the tube and put your feet up—that way you'll be rested *and* you'll be motivated to go extra hard the next day to burn off those 30 grams of milk fat you've sent coursing through your arteries.

Distance Training

Distance training is aerobic base work. It improves cardiac efficiency, increases capillary supply to muscles, increases the size and number of mitochondria in the muscle cells and stimulates their activity in metabolizing both fats and carbohydrates, helps develop coordination (technique), strengthens ligaments and tendons, builds mental "toughness," and basically teaches the body to keep going for long distances for no real reason other than to win a ribbon with a piece of metal stuck to it.

Endurance comes from a combination of relatively high weekly mileage, and from a single long walk at 70-75% of maximum heart rate for anywhere from 90 minutes to four hours. The long walk should make up about 25-30% of weekly mileage, with other endurance walks of shorter duration used to add to overall weekly mileage. These distance walks should be long slow distance (LSD) done at a comfortable, "conversational" pace. Doing them faster gives no additional endurance benefits, and can break the body down if done too often.

Lactate Threshold Training

If you want to race fast, you have to train fast from time to time. Lactate threshold training is fast training, at or near your expected race pace. Threshold workouts have a number of aliases: L.T. workouts, lactate turn-point workouts, anaerobic threshold workouts, or AT workouts are all the same thing. They are training sessions undertaken at a pace or heart rate that is very close to your "lactate threshold"—the speed or heart rate that causes lactic acid to be produced in the muscles at the same rate that your body can break it down. This threshold is determined by blood lactate analysis during training, or can be calculated by plotting heart rate against walking speed and "eyeballing" the deflection point or "turn point" where heart rate begins to level off.

There are several much easier ways to determine the proper pace to walk these workouts:

1. The talk test. Threshold occurs at the point where you can say at most three or four words before having to gasp for air. If you're able to discuss dialectic materialism you're probably going a little too slowly.

2. The Borg test. Threshold occurs at a point where you're in a state of "moderate discomfort" on the Borg scale—a progressive scale of perceived exertion. Your pace should not feel "easy," but not quite painful either.

3. The one-hour test. Threshold equates very closely to the pace a walker can race for fifty minutes to one hour before exhaustion. Many racewalkers can finish an eight- to ten-kilometer race in about an hour, so race pace for these distances corresponds very closely to lactate threshold pace.

Lactate threshold workouts help you to raise your lactate threshold walking speed, enabling you to walk in races at a pace closer to your VO_2 max speed. These are not meant to be killer workouts, so threshold work can and should be done at least once per week, year round. There are two different types of threshold work: lactate threshold intervals and "tempo walks."

Threshold intervals. For 5km and 10km walkers, sessions will generally last between 20 and 50 minutes of total work broken up into five- to 25-minute segments. Recovery between repeats is brief—long enough to ensure that solid technique is maintained, but not so long that heart rate drops precipitously.

Examples are repeat kilometers, repeat miles and repeat 2kms or 3kms with from one to three minutes of rest between each. Repeats can also be done as ascending, descending or up and down "ladders" or "pyramids" such as 400m, 800m, 1,200m, 1,600m, 1,200m, 800m, 400m, with easy 200-meter recoveries between each.

The pace for these repeats should be about 10-15 seconds per kilometer slower than race pace for your primary distance during the off season, and right on race pace as your competition season approaches.

Tempo walks. Occasional fast distance work, especially closer to the competition season is a great way to get really "race-ready," but this type of training can be very stressful. The British refer to these workouts as "speed endurance" sessions, eastern European coaches simply call them "walk IIs," and I call them "tempo walks." Whatever you call them, a good rule of thumb is to approach race distance while approaching race pace. For 5km walkers that means about 4km, for 10km walkers about 8km, and for 20km walkers about 16-18km, all at about 15-30 seconds per km (25-45 seconds per mile) slower than race pace for your primary distance. Heart rate should be sustained at about 85% of maximum. An easy 5km or 10km race can be substituted, but you must have the discipline to hold yourself back. Don't push the pace!

These are so-called "steady-state" tempo workouts. Another variation is an "acceleration tempo." You start the workout at about the same pace you would walk on your long day, but then gradually increase the pace throughout the workout, finishing the last few kilometers at race pace for that distance. This has the effect of taking you through all the stages you would go through during a race, from a relaxed comfortable state to a much more stressful all-out effort in the closing stages.

You should finish any threshold session feeling tired, but with enough energy left so you could theoretically take a short break and then repeat the workout (if somebody put a gun to your head and made you do it.) The danger in this type of workout is that of pushing too hard and killing yourself for the rest of the week's training. Never "smash yourself" in your workouts—gains come not from single super-human efforts, but from consistent long-term training. A single workout will not affect overall conditioning much, but if intensity is too high you can become "overtrained," or worse yet, injured. Save it for the race!

VO_2 Max Training

If your race times have reached a plateau, and you've tried everything else, you *may* want to think about adding some VO_2 max training to your program. Whereas threshold training should be comfortable and controlled, these are killers workouts. They are performed at velocities that force you take up oxygen at absolute peak capacity, with heart rates reaching 95-100% of maximum. There are two variations: VO_2 max intervals and VO_2 max fartlek workouts.

VO2 max intervals. VO2 max intervals consist of very fast two- to seven-minute repeats with equal periods of recovery between each. The fast segments should be walked at a pace between one-mile and 5km race pace, while the recoveries should be a mix of very easy walking and racewalking. The total work load of the fast segments should not exceed 20 to 25 minutes.

One example is a "5x5x5" workout. It consists of five minutes with your heart rate at 90-100% of maximum, followed by five minutes of rest, repeated five times. VO2 work can also be conducted up moderately steep hills to raise heartrate without forcing technique beyond speeds where legality and efficiency can be maintained. These repeats should be limited to about three or four minutes in duration, with an easy walk or jog back down the hill to recover.

VO2 max fartleks. Another type of VO2 max workout is the VO2 max fartlek. Fartlek is Swedish for "speed play," but these workouts are all business: They're sustained workouts with heart rates in the 87-95% of maximum range. After warming up fully, walk for a few minutes at a pace that equates to a heart rate of around 87% of maximum. Then accelerate so that heart rate climbs to the 90-95% range. When fatigue takes over, drop back to the 87% range. Continue doing so for 20-30 minutes.

All VO2 max workouts are stressful to the body and should be used sparingly. Fast intervals also do a lot of muscle damage during the workout itself. You'll need to allow plenty of recovery whenever working at more than 90% of maximum. These workouts do have the potential to increase your race speed by up to 10%—but you need to do your long walks and sustained tempo work first, or all they'll do is break you down.

Too much speed work will also convert aerobic muscle fibers to anaerobic ones. Great if you want to be a world-class 400-meter walker, but since 400-meter racewalk events don't exist, you're better off training to be a 5km to 50km walker. You'll become very fatigued in anything but very short races if you've done too much speed work because those fast-twitch anaerobic muscle fibers create lactic acid as a by-product of energy production. Train for endurance first, then use an occasional VO2 max workout to work on your speed before your important races.

Economy Training

There's only one way to learn to walk fast, and that's by walking fast. Economy repeats *will* get you to walk fast! These sessions, also known as efficiency workouts or rhythm workouts, consist of very fast, but very short repeats that force your technique and physiological systems beyond the point at which they are now operating efficiently. They teach your neuromuscular system to fire very rapidly, maximizing stride rate so you'll feel comfortable at more reasonable speeds—including your race speed. Economy repeats are the fastest walking you'll ever do; even faster than race pace, albeit for much shorter distances. They are bursts of absolute peak to near-peak velocity for 40 to 200 meters, with full recoveries taken between bursts.

The great thing about economy intervals is that they aren't very taxing on the cardiovascular system. They're over with so quickly your heart barely has time to respond. Heart rate will only get up to 85-90% or so, even though you'll be walking faster than race pace.

I usually do a long warm up, then 12 or 16 x 200 meters, or a mix of 100s, 200s and 300s at least once per week to get the life back into my legs after my long day. I may get down to under 6-minute-mile pace, but I actually consider this to be one of my easy days. I'll also do a few short economy intervals as part of my warm-up before any race or threshold workout, and may even throw in a few surges during a long walk to make sure my technique is quick and efficient.

Our limitation will always be how fast we can walk, not how long. We aren't doing six-day races, we're "only" racing 5km to 50km. But before you can walk a fast 5km, or even a fast 50km you must be able to blast a fast 400 meters *efficiently*. Get the speed first, then extend it out to longer and longer distances.

If you learn to walk efficiently and legally at high speed, your lactate threshold pace will be much faster as well, without making any other changes to your training. In fact, economy work will help you to walk more legally, and with less effort, at any pace or distance.

Chapter 9: The "Perfect" Training Schedule

In the previous chapter, five different types of workouts were introduced. The first type was rest and recovery work; each of the four remaining workout types were sessions intended to impart different types of stress to different physiological systems. Every day you should know which type of workout you're about to undertake. If you don't know, don't bother going out the door—you're probably headed for a "junk-mileage" day anyway.

I can't put together one "perfect" training program for every walker. Nobody can, because individuals vary so much in how they respond to training. Some respond to the traditional hard day/easy day approach. Others like to walk two hard days followed by two easy days. But there are several things that make sense physiologically, and seem to work for most people. Among these are:

> **1. You need that long day.** And you need to find time in your week to do it. Whether you're racing 5km or 50km, you need to get out once per week or so to do that easy 15 to 40km walk.

> **2. You need to recover from the long one.** Most walkers should take off at least one day per week to ensure full physical and mental recovery from the week's training. It makes sense to take off after the long day so your muscles can replenish their supply of glycogen and the rest of your body can fully rehydrate and recuperate.

> **3. Economy repeats can really perk you up.** After using relatively "slow" technique during the long walk then taking a day off, you can be left feeling a bit "sluggish." Some nice short, fast economy repeats are guaranteed to put the life back into your legs.

4. You should get in one or two threshold workouts per week. If done properly, threshold workouts should be relatively difficult, but easy enough so that you can handle one or two per week year-round. And it's important that you do, since they are the closest you'll come in training to racing technique and physiology.

5. You need plenty of rest. You can only get in about three really good hard workouts per week. The rest of your training should be easy mileage, cross training or just plain rest days to recover from the hard work.

If these general tenets are followed, there really aren't very many different combinations of the five workout types that can be put together within the framework of a seven-day training week. So the pattern behind the following "Perfect Training Schedule" is appropriate for any racewalker from the beginning 5km competitor to the elite 50km athlete—you simply need to honestly decide where you are in your training.

Beginners will walk four or five days per week, more advanced athletes will walk six. And anyone can "periodize" the schedule (described in chapter 10) by shifting the major focus of the week's workouts throughout the year. During base-building, the major focus will be distance walks, long recovery walks, and economy work. Closer to racing season your focus will shift to a lactate threshold period focusing on less total mileage, but more intensity on threshold days.

I don't write training schedules for athletes unless they are willing to stay in close contact with me so that I can track their progress. Illness, injuries, fatigue and the simple day-to-day distractions that get in the way of training will all necessitate changes to your training schedule; if these changes are not made you run the risk of becoming overtrained. If you're a self-coached walker, you'll need to objectively monitor how your body responds to training. Look for signs of overtraining (chapter 11), and cut back a bit if you think you're overdoing it. If you do have to skip workouts from time to time, read your training log frequently to make sure you're getting in those three or four key workouts per week.

The following schedule is a good start for the self-coached walker. If job or family commitments get in the way of training, you should at least try to get in one Distance day, one Economy day and one or two

Threshold days per week. The rest of the week should be off or easy recovery days. Flexibility is built into the program—you can walk anywhere from 18 to 124 kilometers per week and still be "right on schedule"—it's up to you to decide how much is right for you.

The Perfect Racewalk Training Schedule (For Anybody!)

Day	Sample Workout	Type	Kilometers
M	Off (Easy cross-training is OK)	Recovery	0
T	8-12 x 200 meters FAST with 200 meter rests between each*	Economy	6-12
W	Off or EZ distance (65-75% MHR)	Recovery	0-20
T	20-90 minute steady-state or acceleration tempo walk @ 85% MHR*	Threshold	6-20
F	Off or EZ distance (65-70% MHR)	Recovery	0-20
S	From 3 to 12 x 1km @ race pace (92% MHR) with 2:00 rests between each repeat*	Threshold	6-20
S	Easyish" mileage: Long walk at 70-75% of MHR	Distance	10-32

Total Kilometers: 28-124

*For this and all schedules, it should be understood that all Economy, Tempo and Threshold Workouts begin with a warm-up consisting of 10-20 (or more) minutes of easy walking followed by dynamic flexibility drills. The workouts should be followed by an easy 10-20 minute cool down, then a few minutes of easy stretching. Rests between Threshold Intervals should not exceed 2 minutes.

Carl Schueler on:

Staying Focused: Juggling Career and Athletics

Accomplishments: Four-time Olympian at 50 kilometers (1980, 1984, 1988, 1992). 6th at the 1984 Olympic Games 50km.

Personal Records:
20 kilometers: 1:25:04
35 kilometers: 2:41:26
40 kilometers: 3:03:50
50 kilometers: 3:57:09

Background: Carl "Olympic god" Schueler didn't start racewalking until his sophomore year at Frostburg (Maryland) State University. After graduating, Carl spent four years working as a demographer for the Federal Government before heading off to graduate school at the University of Michigan. In 1983 he moved to Colorado Springs, Colorado to train with the racewalking "colony" at the Olympic Training Center. While there, he began work as a land-use planner for El Paso County—a job he has held ever since. Although he dropped to part-time status in the months leading up to the '80, '84, and '88 Olympics, Carl— now the assistant director of the county planning department—has worked full-time throughout most of his 20-year elite-level racewalking career.

Carl Says: "The most important thing when juggling athletic and other commitments is to make each a separate priority. To succeed in athletics when I was working full-time I tried to keep life simple and to focus on the three to four target workouts I had each week. The rest of the workouts I could be flexible with, but my key workouts were 'written in stone.' I also tried to identify the most efficient way to get my training done, then (usually) just went out and did it before something else got in the way."

Chapter 10: Periodization

It's been extremely gratifying for me to watch budding racewalkers progress by following my "perfect" training schedule. The schedule is a good mix of different workouts that a walker can use to prepare for 5km and 10km races year-round, but eventually, some walkers get *much* better and they begin entertaining thoughts of *peaking* for a few very important races per year instead of trying to be ready for every race on the local calendar. To get into absolute peak condition a few times per year, a racewalker may want to consider *periodization.*

Periodization is a more advanced training system used by athletes wanting to be in top condition one or two times per year during a short competition season or seasons. It's the process of planning a long-term (yearly or quadrennially based) training program broken up into different segments of varying degrees of intensity. The athlete is able to make dramatic improvements by setting long-term competitive goals and systematically training different physiological systems during different periods of the year. After maximum fitness is attained in one physiological system, the gains are maintained while the next system is worked on. The final stage is the sharpening and tapering for the big event.

The goal should be to peak for three or four major races per year, and then to "train through" less important races. A peak can be held for no more than six to eight weeks—attempting to maintain top condition for longer without a rest will ultimately lead to physical and psychological breakdown, so point towards your most important competitions, then allow the body to fully recover before building up to the next race.

The biggest downside to periodization is that there will necessarily be times during the year when you'll be in a base-building or rest phase in which you're not going to be in very good racing shape. That's why you'll often see some of the best racewalkers walking relatively slow times during off-season races. But the benefits in terms of time improvements during the "up" phases far outweigh the inconvenience of having to lay low during the rebuilding phases.

The Five Periods

Most athletes break the training cycle into four or five periods, focusing on a particular type of workout during each phase. The terminology will vary, but I go by the following: active-rest, base-building, a *very* optional VO2 max period, a pre-competition lactate threshold period, and the competition period.

1. Active-rest period. Months of training and a long racing season can leave you feeling pretty beat up, both physically and mentally. After your last big race, you need to shut down for a while to let yourself recover. Assuming your big races are in the summer and early fall, begin your next training cycle with an active-rest period lasting from four to eight weeks. Use this time to enjoy some cross training. Long autumn hikes and bike rides are great for endurance, as is cross-country skiing. (You might want to substitute roller blading if you live below the snow belt.) Stay active though—don't lose your earlier gains. Once you're fully recovered and raring to go, you'll start up again with an endurance/economy base-building phase.

2. Base-building period. This is what it's all about. Racewalking is an aerobic event, so the only way to consistently improve is to do a lot of aerobic training. Base-building should be a mix of long endurance walks, easy recovery walks, and frequent economy sessions to retain efficient technique. Occasional tempo walks are also beneficial.

The base-building phase will be the longest period, lasting up to six months or more. The distance of the long day or days will vary depending on the primary race distance, and will increase as time goes by. 5km walkers should build up to a long day of about 15km, 10km walkers should work up to 20km and 20km walkers should be out for 30km on the longest day of the week. If brain damage has set in and you want to walk a marathon or 50km, you'll need to occasionally get out for as long as 35 to 40 kilometers. If at all possible, you should also walk one or two additional "longish" days per week. These should be about 5km shorter and perhaps slightly faster than your longest day.

Rebuild your mileage base gradually—increases in the distance of the long walk or walks, and increases in total weekly mileage should be limited to 10% per week. Pace of the endurance workouts should also be increased gradually, and only after a comfortable mileage plateau has been reached. Work on increasing either distance or pace at any particular time, but not both.

One or two economy repeat workouts per week, usually a few days after the long day will keep the legs fast and fresh. It's also not a bad idea to throw an occasional 30- or 60-second acceleration or some quick-step drills into your long walks to keep your legs alive.

3. VO2 max period. Again, this is an optional period for "advanced" athletes only. It's a transitional phase to get the body ready for the heavy emphasis on lactate threshold work to follow. Since lactate threshold can be measured as a certain percentage of VO2 max, if VO2 max rises so too will threshold. The idea is to bump up the max values so that threshold—at about 90% of maximum—will also rise.

Some athletes do blistering intervals on the track to achieve gains in VO2 max, but I don't recommend that any sane person do so. A much better solution is to do the intervals on hills. The hills will assuredly get your heart pounding, but at much lower walking speeds. The result is increased cardiac power and more leg strength with less damage to the hamstrings and other leg muscles. Try to find a relatively long hill, steep enough to be difficult, but not so steep that it ruins your technique. Do six to eight repeats of between one and four minutes in duration, with any easy walk or jog back down the hill for recovery.

Don't do any more than two VO2 max sessions per week. One of them can actually be an extension of your economy workout—simply increase the distance of the intervals to 400-600 meters at close to the same pace, with recoveries at least as long as the time it takes to do the interval. A long day and easy recovery walks will round out the rest of the week's training.

4. Lactate threshold period. This is a four- to six-week pre-competitive period where the focus shifts to frequent tempo walks and lactate threshold "pace" intervals to get your body used to the rigors of walking at a sustained fast paces. As the weeks go by, you should build up to two or three threshold or tempo workouts per week, fitting them in on the days where you would normally do your VO2 and economy sessions. Closer to races, cut mileage and concentrate on sharpening speed. One long endurance session every two weeks will be sufficient to maintain your hard-earned base-fitness level.

5. Competitive period. A one- to two-week "taper" should be used to help you peak for your major races. A taper, discussed more fully in chapter 12, is a short period of rest and sharpening before each race. Weekly distance should drop to anywhere from two thirds to one third of "normal" levels, but *intensity should remain high* to retain sharpness. Don't turn into a couch potato—you must continue to walk fast and with excellent technique in the days before your races.

If you're competing in more than one race during the competitive period, keep your mileage at 2/3 to 1/2 of normal levels, mixing abbreviated threshold and economy workouts with rest days. If you have two or more weeks between races, try to fit in long days on the weekends to maintain your endurance base.

How to Schedule 'em

1. Mark your calendar. When are your key races and how fast do you want to walk in those races? Periodization is a very effective way to plan workouts so that all physiological systems are running at 100% on important race days. To map out an effective training schedule you must have concrete performance goals, and know when those big races are. When you've decided which races to key on, mark them on the calendar.

2. Plan your taper. To begin the periodization process count back seven to 14 days before your goal race or races—this is your *taper* period. The idea is to be rested while maintaining high VO_2 and lactate threshold levels. Maintain your usual training schedule, but cut total mileage and number of intervals by 1/3 to1/2.

3. Work in a lactate threshold phase. Count back three to six weeks before your taper. This is your lactate threshold period. Your main focus should be on raising your lactate threshold walking speed—the speed beyond which high levels of lactate begin to accumulate in the muscles and blood. Training should consist of two to three lactate threshold interval or tempo sessions per week in addition to the long day and the usual recovery/technique sessions.

4. *Maybe* add a VO2 max period. If you really think you're ready, schedule in a short, one- to three-week, VO2 max period before the threshold period. Raising VO2 max will increase your ability to take in oxygen while walking at high speed. Fartlek workouts at 87 to 95% of max heart rate and interval and hill workouts at 95 to 100% of max heart rate should be undertaken two times per week during this period. Be conservative—don't even think about using a VO2 max period unless you've been walking competitively for at least two years.

5. Schedule a *long* base period. Before your VO2 max or threshold period count back as long as you have available—three to nine months or more. This is your endurance base buildup/economy period. Your main focus will be building general and racewalking-specific endurance, as well as developing solid economical technique. Whereas lactate threshold and VO2 max improvements constitute primarily enzymatic changes, improvements in endurance represent structural changes: increased capillary supply to the muscles, increased size and number of mitochondria within the muscles, strengthening of ligaments and tendons, etc. These structural changes take a great deal of time to develop, as does good technique—and without these changes, lactate threshold and VO2 max work will be counterproductive or damaging; take the time to lay down a solid foundation of base work.

6. Plan your rest period. Finally, before the endurance/economy mix base period there is a two- to four-week active-rest phase. After each hard racing season the body must be given a chance to recover. Racewalking should be severely cut back or eliminated. Fitness gains will be maintained by pursuing alternate activities like biking, roller-blading, swimming or hiking. Choose activities that you enjoy that you've neglected during your hard training and racing seasons. Have fun! Give yourself a full physical and mental recovery before embarking on the next season's training.

The following is a sample periodized calendar for a masters walker wanting to perform at his best at the World Veterans Championships and the National Masters Track and Field Championships in July, and the National Masters 5km and the Casimiro Alongi Memorial 5km in September. He also plans to use a few pre-season races in March as "tune-ups" to check his progress.

Periodized Calendar Targeting June/July and September Peaks

Nov.	Dec.	Jan.	Feb.	Mar.	Apr.	May	June	July	Aug.	Sep.	Oct.
Endurance/economy mix				Early season races	Threshold		Taper	Main Season	Endurance and threshold mix	Mini season	Active Rest
4 to 6 months				1 month	4 to 6 weeks		10 days	4 to 6 weeks	5 to 6 weeks	3 to 4 weeks	1 month

Chapter 11: A Few Words on Overtraining

Although you definitely need to work hard to become a good racewalker, it is possible to overdo it. Don't be a bonehead—it's always much better to go into a race marginally undertrained than overtrained. Improvements come from adapting to reasonable stresses. Consistent, intelligent training leads to success; over-stress without recovery does nothing but make you tired. Doing too much will eventually lead to illness, injury and "flat" performances.

Over Racing

"Over racing" is as bad as overtraining. Try not to race too often, but if you must compete frequently, don't treat every race like it's the Olympics. You can't be "up" for every competition—if you try to do so you'll walk yourself into the ground. If you're lucky enough to have frequent races on your local calendar pick the ones that are the most important to you and key for them. Use the others as tempo walks, but don't push too hard!

If you don't have the self-control to hold back, volunteer to work registration or results, but leave those racing shoes at home. Whenever I help out at a local race I always make sure I leave my walking shoes at home so I won't be tempted to take off when I hear the gun go off. Of course it's no guarantee that I won't at least *try* to race—I've "blown-out" a lot of sandals that way, but having a flip-flop explode into shreds 20 meters into a race is usually enough to make me stop racewalking, so I guess the strategy works.

Warning Signs

Signs of overtraining are: sudden unexplained weight loss, loss of enthusiasm or drive, irritability, changes in sleeping habits or insomnia, loss of appetite, loss of libido, excessive thirst, swollen glands and high morning pulse rate. Of course that also sounds a lot like malaria, rabies, or a variety of other maladies, but even if it is rabies or some nasty tropical disease, you should *still* take the day off.

Use your training log to gauge how well you're recovering from your training. Weigh yourself, and take resting pulse rate every morning—if your morning heart rate is more than 10% higher than usual or if you're loosing weight *too* suddenly, take an easy day—or better yet, a day off—no matter what your schedule says. You're probably fatigued, dehydrated and on the verge of a breakdown. Or perhaps it's just a touch of that Ebola virus that's been going around....

Chapter 12: Peaking

Most racewalkers, either through trial and error or by design, eventually settle on a training schedule that works best for them. Unfortunately, many of these same walkers become bewildered in the final weeks and days before an important race, either training too much or too little. Another common problem is failure to specifically prepare the body and mind for conditions they will likely experience during competition.

Whether your training philosophy tends towards periodization, or towards a consistent year-round training program, peaking for important races is crucial. According to Canadian coach, Dr. Tudor Bompa, peaking is "...a temporary state of training produced when physical and psychological elements are maximized and when the levels of technical and tactical preparation are optimal." Peaking is the scheduling of training by a racewalker leading up to the most important competitions of the year in such a way as to ensure optimum performance.

Trust Your Training

For better or worse, whatever training you've done in the months before a race will rise to the top on race day—but only if you allow it to. You must have faith in your fitness going into a race—don't undermine your training by hammering yourself in the last week. Additional fitness gains will be minimal, and they will be overshadowed by the detriment of going into the race fatigued.

There is such a thing as "training through" less-important races, but doing so will sacrifice your best possible performance in these races in exchange for higher-quality training for future, presumably more important competitions. If you want to perform at your absolute peak now, however, you must be rested. But what does "rested" mean?

Tapering

Assuming that you have trained rigorously, a taper is a way of resting both physically and mentally before an important competition without losing any of the fitness gained during the preceding months of training. This does not mean a complete layoff from training. Quite the contrary: An effective taper is characterized by high intensity training, albeit at lower volume than in the previous weeks. This has traditionally meant maintaining much the same schedule in the final two weeks before the race, except with a 1/3 to 1/2 reduction in both the number of intervals, and in total weekly mileage.

When tapering, remember that rest, glycogen storage, enzymatic adaptation, and improved economy are the goals. Mileage should be reduced to the lowest possible level to ensure that the legs are rested and fully glycogen loaded, while still doing a limited number of fast economy intervals. The time for hard mileage has passed—the final week should feel very easy, leaving you "champing at the bit" for a fast race. If in doubt, always do less!

A typical taper for a 65-kilometers (40-miles) per-week walker preparing for a 5km race is as follows:

Sunday: Easy 10 kilometers with between four and six 30-second accelerations thrown in during the walk.

Monday: Off. Perhaps swim for 20 minutes or soak in a Jacuzzi, then stretch.

Tuesday: Easy 45-minute racewalk.

Wednesday: 2km warm up, then 2 x 1km @ 5km race pace with a 1-minute rest between them. Cool down, then stretch.

Thursday: Easy 45 minute racewalk.

Friday: 2km warm up, then 6 x 400 meters @ 5km race pace with 1-minute rests between each. Cool down, then stretch.

Saturday: 20-minute warm up on the race course, then 4 x 50 meter accelerations. Cool down, then stretch.

Sunday: Personal Record Race!

Super Taper?

Recent research indicates that an even greater reduction in mileage may be beneficial both in the short term and over longer periods to give your base training a boost. Owen Anderson, writing in *Running Research News,* discusses studies with runners who used no taper, a traditional taper, and a taper characterized by drastic reductions in total mileage, and a limited number of short, high-intensity intervals every day in the week leading up to the race.

These intervals—run at slightly faster than 5km race pace—amounted to only 15% of the runners' usual weekly mileage in the final week, with enough easy mileage added to ensure sufficient warm ups and cool downs. For racewalkers training 40 miles per week, this would amount to about six miles of intervals in the week before the race. The bulk of these intervals should be completed in the first few days of the taper, with the number of intervals declining through the week. About 800 meters warm up and 800 meters cool down should be incorporated into each workout, increasing total mileage for the week to about 13 miles. This may seem like a ridiculously low mileage total for the week, but remember the primary purpose of the taper: Rest!

The group of runners utilizing the very low mileage, high-intensity taper realized a 6% increase in economy over both the regular taperers and the non-taperers. The average time improvement amounted to 29 seconds over 5km, with every runner in the group improving. Anderson attributed the increase to both the enhanced rest as well as the benefits of the up-tempo running.

What does this mean to the racewalker? Such a taper, coupled with copious stretching and rest should mean enhanced flexibility, more economical technique, increased enzymatic activity and glycogen storage in the leg muscles and quite possibly surprisingly fast race times while doing less work. I've tried this approach on several occasions and was rewarded with solid performances each time.

Whichever taper you decide to use, remember that building endurance and sharpening speed take many months of hard work. Last-minute attempts to "catch up" on missed training will only make you tired, so be sure to get plenty of rest in the days before your big competitions; once you've done your hard training, the "rest" is easy.

Chapter 13: Marathon Training

Finishing a marathon can be an experience of a lifetime. And if your goal is to "simply" go the distance, the training can be fairly painless. But if you want to *race* the marathon, you'll need to be extremely focused in your preparation.

Marathon training is really a book unto itself, so I can't cover all the bases here, but the tips and schedule below will get you to the finish line in one piece. Additionally, if you're seriously considering walking a marathon, the Leukemia and Lymphoma Society's "Team in Training" program (described in Appendix II) is a great option. You'll get qualified coaching, other walkers to train with and an all-expense-paid trip to a marathon in an exotic location.

Although quality 20km training can prepare you adequately for the marathon, the race itself is a whole different animal from the 20. You absolutely, positively have to get those long days in, and you must limit the intensity of your speed days. If you hammer your speed work, your glycogen supply will run out miles before the finish line: Can you say "Hitting The Wall?" You don't need all-out speed, you need to be able to maintain a more reasonable pace for a very long distance. So long tempo walks—in the 25km (15.5 mile) range—will become key workouts.

Assuming that you're already comfortable walking at least 15km (9.3 miles) once per week, the long-day mileage build-up leading up to a marathon should begin about 20 weeks before the race. You'll need to focus on building up the distance of the long day to between 20 miles and 35km (21.7 miles). There's no reason to do the entire 42km (26.2 miles) in training, but it's imperative to get in at least three 30-35km workouts before the race.

Tapering is equally important: Your last very long (25-35km) workout should be at least two weeks—and preferably three weeks—before the competition. Don't try to squeeze in one last long walk the week marathon; the extra effort will only leave you fatigued and depleted.

I've put a whole lot more detail in *The Complete Guide to Marathon Walking,* but the following is a typical marathon training schedule, including the long-day mileage buildup:

Marathon Training Schedule

Day	Base-Building	Threshold	Taper
M	Off	Off	Off
T	Economy: 10-12 x 200 meters fast with easy 200-meter rests or 3-4 x (100, 200, 300) fast with easy 100-meter rests	20 x 400 meters @ 5 seconds faster than marathon pace, w/ 1:00 rests between each	1/2 Economy: 6 x 200 meters or 4 x 400 meters with 200-meter rests
W	Easy 10-15 kilometers	Easy 45 minutes	Easy 30 minutes
T	Off or easy 30-45 minutes walking or cross training	Tempo walk: 15-20km acceleration tempo or steady-state tempo on alternate weeks	Tempo: Easy 10 mins., fast 10 mins., easy 10 mins.
F	Tempo walk: 15-20km steady-state or acceleration tempo on alternate weeks	Off or easy 30-45 minutes	Easy 20 minutes
S	Easy 30-45 minutes	8 x 2km or 5-6 x 3km @ marathon pace with 2-3:00 rests	Easy 20 mins. warm up, dynamic flexibiltiy drills, then 4 x 30 seconds fast. Then stretch.
S	Long-day: Follow 15-32 km long-day progression outlined below.		Marathon!

Distance progression of the long day, starting 20 weeks before the marathon:

15km, 18km, 15km, 20km, 15km, 22km, 18km, 25km, 20km, 28km, 23km, 30km, 25km, 30km, 25km, 32km, 25km, 32km, 25km, 15km, Marathon

Herm Nelson on:

Secrets of Marathon and 50km Training

Accomplishments: 1992 and 1996 Olympian at 50km. Former American track record holder at 30km (2:21:40), 40km (3:31:58) and 50km (3:59:41). 1995 U.S. Olympic Festival Gold Medalist and Penn Relays 10km Champion.

Personal Records:
5 kilometers: 20:09
10 kilometers: 42:05
20 kilometers: 1:26:47
50 kilometers: 3:59:41

Background: Herm, from Seattle Washington, started running marathons as a 12-year-old to spend time with his father who was an avid runner. Herm ran two marathons in the sixth grade with a best of 4:10:02. By the end of ninth grade he had run eight more with a best of 3:02:49. After high school Herm attended the U.S. Naval Academy at Annapolis, and then Western Washington University, where he was introduced to racewalking in 1986. He was 7th at the 1988 National 50km, and 5th at the 1988 Olympic 50km Trials 9 weeks later—only 18 months after learning to racewalk. Herm went on to make the '92 and '96 Olympic Teams, and to set the American Record for 50km on his home track in Seattle in 1996.

Herm Says: "After achieving a string of early successes, it seemed like the sky was the limit, but eventually one hits a plateau, and walking 50kms repeatedly brings with it a high potential for injury. A series of injuries slowed my progress a lot since 1989, but the accomplishments have continued to trickle in so I have kept competing. If one wants to improve as a competitive walker, the primary object of the game is avoiding injury. Racing fast and avoiding injury are kind of engineering opposites, like designing a car with both good performance and good fuel economy.

"When training for 50km, my mileage peaks at 100-110 miles per week. At that level I don't fully recover from my workouts until I begin my taper approximately 2 weeks before the race. That is the secret to preparing well for 50km; it is what [Australian coach and Olympian] Simon Baker refers to as 'maintaining a base fatigue level'. You teach your body to walk efficiently in speed and long tempo workouts while you are trashed. You have to do everything you can to recover—swimming, Jacuzzi, chiropractic, self-massage—but that just allows you to stuff more work into your schedule, not to be fresher.

"The single litmus test to show whether you are doing it right or not is if you are able to hold to target paces from one hard workout to the next, or whether you croak. If you are fast in one or two workouts, and then you croak in the next one, you are not ready to handle the workload. Usually the problem can be solved with additional base mileage. The trick is to do it without getting injured, and it's a fine line between doing it and overdoing it when you train right for 50km."

Chapter 14: Rules to Live By

One of the most important elements of effective racewalk training is consistency. Top U.S. walkers aren't competing with the rest of the world (yet!) because we don't have the single-minded focus that our overseas counterparts have. Most elite American racewalkers know how to train—and we do quite well for months at a time—but we're too easily distracted by the craziness of our 21st-century American lifestyle and fail to maintain a consistent high level of training over a period of years rather than months.

To succeed you need to put yourself on a program to achieve your goals and stick to it. If you know "The Rules" and how your body works, you can build a program that will allow you to train smarter—not necessarily harder— and take minutes off your best times. Some of these rules are:

> **1. Think long-term.** Set your race schedule months in advance. Target specific races, using others along the way as training sessions, pick ambitious but realistic goals, then plot out a course to work towards them. Make sure every workout has a purpose towards attaining these goals. In other words: Have a plan.

> **2. Train consistently.** Don't fall into the trap of training maniacally for a few weeks followed by several weeks of half-hearted training: Stick to the plan.

> **3. Give it a chance.** Adaptation takes time. It takes three to six weeks for the human body to adapt to a particular physiological stress. Don't increase training load, or switch to a different focus (e.g., from endurance to lactate threshold) more often than this. During a particular cycle keep most of the variables constant. If you're increasing distance, don't increase pace and *vice versa*. After three to six weeks make the change, but allow the body to adapt to each higher level first before moving on.

4. Stress is stress. Your body doesn't know good stress from bad stress. If you try to counter a hard day at work with a hard day on the track, you're asking for a breakdown. Training suffers if you have a life; give in to the fact instead of trying to fight it. You'll be better off physically, emotionally, and your marriage will last longer. If you have a very stressful day, adjust your workouts accordingly. Remember common sense: Get plenty of sleep, eat right, and relax—this is supposed to be fun!

5. Limit the speed. Racewalking is an aerobic activity! Excessive speed work WILL teach you to walk fast over short distances, but it will also teach your body to rely on lactate-producing fast-twitch muscle fibers. What does that mean? You're going to die in the middle of your next 5km race.

6. Variety is the spice of training. Most athletes don't do what they need to do, they do what they're good at. Rely on your strengths, but work hard to improve your weaknesses. If you do nothing but easy mileage, think about mixing in some speed work. If you do lots of track work, get out on the roads for more distance work.

7. Hard is hard, easy is easy. If you don't take it really easy on the easy days, you'll be too tired to go hard on the hard days—and yes, you do have to go hard on the hard days! How's this for a paradox? The faster the race, the slower you need to go on your long days and recovery days. If you're racing mostly 5kms, you should be hammering on the track and taking it really easy on the roads. If you're training for the marathon, however, the separation between hard and easy won't be as great: You'll go pretty easy on your "speed" days, but push the pace a little more on your long workouts.

8. Take small steps. Don't increase mileage by more than 10% per week.

9. Taper for big races. From one to three weeks before a major competition cut mileage to allow the body to rest. Do not neglect speed though! Include a few short, fast sessions to maintain leg speed while resting up. I usually like to go out and do a fast, but reduced-mileage lactate threshold session two to four days before a race, and then a very limited economy session the night before (6 x 50 meters). These leave the legs fresh and fast, and according to some sources they have the effect of super-oxygenating the blood. I just know that they make me feel good the next day.

10. When in doubt, rest. It's always better to do too little training than to do too much. Alternate hard days with easy days, take a day off every once in a while, and taper going into races. Remember: Overtraining is wasted training.

If Want to Walk Fast You Have to Walk Slow

While at the University of Virginia finishing my masters, I often ran into Bill Burke while doing distance workouts on a marked course in the rural "Horse Country" surrounding Charlottesville. Bill, then getting a law degree at UVA, was a few years earlier the first Princeton student to ever break four minutes for the mile. One day Bill asked if I'd like to join him some day for one of his easy 10-mile workouts—his long day. Excited by the prospect of running with one of the rising stars of middle distance running in the U.S., I agreed.

Since Bill was still relatively new to Charlottesville, I decided to show him one of my favorite courses on a nature trail adjacent to a municipal golf course. We agreed to meet about four days later. Since I figured I was representing all racewalkers everywhere, I wanted to make a good impression. I guessed that "easy" to Bill meant 5:30 or 6-minute miles, so I canceled my 30km workout that week, cut my mileage way back and ran some 400-meter repeats to get ready—I was in serious training for this "easy" workout!

When The Day finally came, I was ready. I figured I could hang on for the whole ten miles if we didn't go under six-minute pace, but I knew I'd be dead after five or six miles if we did 5:30s. We started off with an easy jog at about eight minutes per mile. I remember praying that this warm up would count towards the 10 miles. One mile became two, two became three, so finally after about four miles I asked when we were going to pick up the pace. Bill just laughed and said if I wanted to run fast I could join him for some 52-second quarter-mile repeats the next day, but on his easy days he ran EASY. Here was a guy who went on to win the 1995 USATF National Championship at 1,500 meters; a guy who could run a mile in under four minutes, doing his training runs at 8:00 pace—the equivalent of a sub-6:00 racewalker doing distance work at 12:00 pace.

I used to try to make sure all my training was under 8:30 pace—if I was too tired to keep the pace up I'd take the day off. But now, although I don't do my easy walks as slow as 12:00 pace, if I really need to recover from a hard effort I don't worry if the pace falls back to a leisurely 9:30 or 10:00 mile. This way I'm able to go much faster on my hard days, and my weekly mileage is twice what it was before. The moral of the story: If you want to race fast, separate the easy days from the hard days.

Chapter 15: Common Training Mistakes

Even if you try to follow the rules, it's easy to fall into traps. Here are some common mistakes beginning (and elite!) walkers often make.

1. Going too fast on easy days. Hard training without sufficient recovery is wasted training. Pushing the pace on easy days, or doing too many miles on these days will leave you less than ready for the hard days and, before long, overtrained.

2. Going too fast on threshold repeats. Racewalking races are aerobic races. Walking more than 10% faster than race pace will train convertible muscle fibers to produce energy anaerobically instead of aerobically. You'll be fast over very short distances, but you'll be swimming in lactate half way through your 5km and 10km races.

3. Going too fast on long days. Are you seeing a pattern here? Long days are meant to teach the body to work aerobically by replicating mitochondria, capillarizing muscles, and converting muscle fibers to aerobic energy production. Walking faster doesn't make these changes happen any faster, and it can be very damaging to the muscles you're trying to develop. Occasional long fast days are a part of 20km and 50km training, but doing them too frequently will lead to burnout.

4. Lack of variety in training. You need to call upon a number of different physiological systems when racing. If you don't train them all consistently, you'll be unprepared to race.

5. Insufficient rest. It's great to be excited about racewalking and to want to work hard to improve, but the body can only take so much stress. You need to temper the hard work with sufficient rest to allow full recovery. Keep a close watch for the signs of overtraining. If you're starting to feel ragged, take a day off. If you're working hard but your race times are getting worse, it means you need less, not more hard work.

Chapter 16: On Being Your Own Coach

If you had a great racewalking coach guiding your day-to-day training, would you be reading this book right now? Of course you would! (Sorry, trick question.) But most racewalkers resort to books and videos not because they've stumbled across the greatest racewalking book and video in the English language, they do so because they don't have a good racewalking coach to guide them. So they fumble around, hunting down information wherever they can find it, eventually accumulating a pile of both good and bad resources without knowing which ones to trust and which ones to toss out with last month's leftover lasagna.

Only You Know You

If you take the time to learn all you can about the sport, being your own coach can have its advantages. Nobody knows your body and your daily habits better than you. Except maybe the weird guy with the binoculars across the street, but that's another story entirely. Even if you're a full-time racewalker—and who is?—life can get in the way of your training. Throw into the mix family and work commitments, and unexpected illnesses and injuries, and you have an untenable situation if you're trying to adhere to a concrete training schedule.

To really benefit from a coach, he has to be there every day to monitor your workouts and how you're responding to them. If your coach isn't there for you, he may not know if you're overtraining (or undertraining) until it's too late. If you know what each type of workout is supposed to do for you and you know how to monitor your body, you'll be able to make the adjustments on your own.

It does help to have someone to objectively monitor your training, though—even if the monitor doesn't know much about racewalking. It can be hard to admit to yourself that you're doing too much, so ask someone if it makes sense to double your mileage the week before a race, or to drag the rear axle of a Volkswagen Bug behind you when training. Even crazy ol' Aunt Eunice will tell you that you're out of your mind!

Be Flexible

When I'm not training for anything in particular and life gets a little crazy I'll write myself very loose schedules that incorporate the key workouts I need to walk within a one- or two-week period, but in no particular order. I'll fit the important ones in when I have the time, and just do easy recovery workouts on my really busy days. The same program might work for you. Set your training goals for the week, make sure you get in the two or three important hard days, then let your body and your time schedule work out the details.

Another approach is to write out the coming week's workouts after you know what your non-training commitments are going to be. If you have a meeting on Wednesday that's going to cut into your training time, don't plan your long day for Wednesday. Put the hard workouts on days where you have enough time to get in a good workout, stretching, etc., then build the rest of the week's training around those key workouts.

Keep a Training Log

After training for a while, certain patterns will usually become apparent. You may find that you feel great the day after a threshold workout, but lousy two days later. Or maybe you have a hard time getting through your long workouts if you push too hard the day before. Everybody responds to training differently.

Your own personal history will teach you what works best for you, but memory alone isn't sufficient—you have to write it down! Keeping close track of your workouts in your training diary is the only way you'll ever be able to develop your own individual set of training "rules." Writing down your workouts every day can also keep you from "slacking off." By logging your workouts you become much more aware of whether or not you're really doing everything you need to do to reach your goals. One day off can often turn into two, and two into three if you fail to record your workouts.

A training log can be anything from a page where you record your daily mileage walked, to a true diary where you record your thoughts and feelings along with your goals, mileage, course, pace per km or mile, weather, heart rate data, morning weight and heart rate, what you eat, and anything else you can think of that may affect your performance. Keeping track of such variables allows you to see your improvements over time, and enables you to learn from your successes and failures which training methods work for you and which don't.

Read through your log before each race to build up your confidence. You've done the training necessary to compete well haven't you? Of course you have; it's all there in black and white. After the race read back to see what went right or wrong: If you've done a lot of long slow distance, you're probably strong but possibly not reaching your speed potential. You probably need more threshold and VO_2 work. If you felt fast, but you "crashed" at the end of the race, you probably needed more distance. If you felt that your technique held you back, you may need more economy work.

Seek Out Help

Being your own coach doesn't mean you shouldn't continue to try to learn everything you can about the sport. Read books, watch videos—especially competition tapes of fast, legal athletes—and seek out advice from top coaches and athletes.

Having said that, don't change your training program or technique every two weeks with every new article you read or "expert" you talk to. Stick with what works, especially if your times are still coming down. Only seek to change what clearly isn't working.

Final Thoughts

In a perfect world we would all have great coaches, unlimited time to train, and there would be time for a nap, a Jacuzzi, and a nice relaxing massage after every workout. Unfortunately, that's not the case for most of us. If you can't find a good coach, you need to take control of your own training. That means scheduling a variety of "hard" workouts to train each of your physiological systems, then being smart enough to do everything you can do to facilitate recovery: rest and recovery days; plenty of sleep, including naps if you can fit them in; massage, chiropractic and other body work; and swimming, Jacuzzi, sauna and steam sessions if you have access to these facilities.

Even if you do have a coach, you need to monitor your recovery by watching for signs of overtraining. Take your resting pulse rate, and weigh yourself each morning; and look out for prolonged bouts of muscle soreness and loss of enthusiasm in your training. Listen to your body, use your training log, and take good care of yourself before there's a problem, and you'll walk faster—much faster—with less effort and fewer injuries.

SECTION III: PSYCHOLOGY

THE ELUSIVE 3rd ELEMENT SEPARATING SUCCESS AND FAILURE

It's very difficult to separate the three elements of racewalking preparation: technique, training and psychology, because psychology weaves itself through all elements of training and competition. For example, you must focus on technique *while* training, which requires concentration; a psychological tool. Although I'm hardly an expert in sports psychology, I have learned a few things over the years from some of the experts in the field during our National Team training camps at the U.S. Olympic Training Centers, and in classes I've taken with world-renowned sports psychologists at the University of Virginia.

I've learned a lot about goal setting, relaxation, and visualization techniques, but to me the most important aspect of sports psychology is simple motivation. To excel you need to train. When it's raining or snowing you have to get out the door anyway. Sometimes you need to be a little creative, but you still need to do the workouts. During summers in LaGrange, Georgia or Mobile, Alabama it's just too hot and humid to do good tempo workouts outdoors, so I'll often do them on a treadmill. If you think it's tough to hammer for two hours out on the roads, try it indoors on a treadmill—trust me on this one, it "builds character."

This section will talk a bit about the importance of goals, mental toughness, concentration and relaxation in racewalk training and competition.

Chapter 17: Goal Setting

The mind can be one of the most important weapons in a racewalker's arsenal. It can also be his worst enemy. Monetary or other rewards are very sparse in the sport, so intrinsic motivation and non-tangible rewards are really all there is to keep you going. To stay motivated you need *concrete* goals. These goals should be ambitious enough to provide motivation, yet realistic enough to be attainable with proper training. Sometimes, when the going gets tough, training well can become a game of mind over matter. There's nobody forcing you out the door when the weather gets ugly—you have to believe in your goals and your training plan and not let externalities like the weather get in your way.

Having a concrete goal in mind is often the only thing preventing you from spending the evening with Ben and Jerry instead of Lefty and Righty, your walking shoes.

Commitment

Commitment to what you're doing is the key to achieving your goals. Sometimes it can be hard to train consistently when your target race is months away, but you need to "keep your eye on the ball." Long-term focus and faith in the program will get you through the hard training and to the starting line prepared to excel. That faith in the program is also what gives you the "common sense" and self-confidence to take a day off when needed, or the courage to get through tough workouts. Then, before an important race, you can look back on those months of training and have faith that you are ready.

The simple fact that you're reading this book shows a certain amount of commitment. But to achieve ambitious goals, you need to really make racewalking an important part of your life. You need to make decisions in your life based on how the outcome will affect your training and racing. Obviously you should choose the option that will help rather than hurt your walking. Should you stay up to watch the "America's Funniest Home Videos Three-Hour Special" or go to bed so you can train in the morning? Do you keep a pair of training shoes in the car or take them on business trips, or do you use not having them as an excuse to not train? Do you take the elevator instead of the stairs, the car instead of walking or bicycling? Should you eat that bacon double cheeseburger before or after your workout?

You can't just be a racewalker or an athlete one or two hours a day while you're training. You have to have an athlete's mentality, an athlete's *commitment* 24 hour a day, every day to be your best.

Individualize Your Goals

Commitment comes from believing that your goals are worthy, and believing that they are attainable. Television drills into our heads the idea that if you come in second you're a loser; that an Olympic silver medalist should be apologetic. But it's not realistic for most people to set their goals at the Olympic medal level. Most elite racewalkers don't even have winning an Olympic gold medal as a goal—only three walkers on the planet can do so within any four-year period (two if Korzienowski decides to double!). So it's not realistic for *everybody* to have that goal. But whatever your goals may be, you need to believe that they are worthy, and that you have what it takes to achieve them.

Success doesn't always mean winning the race. It is a very individual thing, and it can mean anything, from setting a personal record to beating a rival, or just finishing a race feeling good and maintaining efficient technique.

These are *your* goals; what's important is that they are important to *you*. It helps to be surrounded by supportive people who care about you and your goals, but often we have to train and race in anonymity. This is about *you*. If the local paper doesn't want to write about racewalking or your co-workers don't understand what you're doing, $©π≅Ψ 'em. What matters is that *you* believe what you're doing is important.

Evaluation

After each competition assess your situation. If you've achieved your objectives, decide where to go from there. If not, evaluate what went wrong. Look back in your training log: Were you undertrained? Overtrained? Was the initial goal overly ambitious? Or was your "failure" simply caused by something beyond your control? Perhaps bad weather, or a competitor's superior performance.

If you didn't reach your goal, either train harder, or "lower the bar" a bit—make sure the new goal is still challenging, but maybe a bit more realistic than your prior, unmet goal. If, however, you did achieve your goal, congratulate yourself, but don't rest on your laurels. Set your sights on new, loftier goals, then map out a course to achieve them.

Curt Clausen on:

Mental Preparation for Racewalkers

Accomplishments: 1996 Olympian and Olympic Trials Champion at 20 kilometers. 1997 National 20km Champion and IAAF World Championships Team member. 2000 Olympic and Olympic Trials Champion at 50 kilometers. American record-holder at many distances.

Personal Records:
1 mile: 5:51.61
5 kilometers: 19:35
10 kilometers: 40:47
20 kilometers: 1:23:34
50 kilometers: 3:48:04

Background: Born in Trenton, New Jersey, Curt grew up in Wisconsin where he began racewalking for the Stevens Point Area Running Club as a 7th grader. After graduating from Duke University and North Carolina State University with degrees in Public Policy Studies and Public Administration, Curt began work as an administrative analyst for the town of Chapel Hill. Often required to work late hours at the office, Curt would sometimes do hard 2-hour walks at under eight-minute-mile pace on his home treadmill. 2 hours on a treadmill? That's mental toughness!

Curt Says: "I believe that mental preparation is the key element that determines the outcome of most races—it is the difference between winning and losing. Proper mental preparation can also help the athlete break through artificial barriers (e.g., mental) and set new personal bests that once seemed impossible. And on the more mundane side, it can help insure the athlete gets out the door on a day to day basis to train effectively. What is proper mental preparation? I think this depends upon the individual and must be discovered through trial and error. Techniques that I have found effective for me include:

    1. Goal Setting. Dreaming of what can be.
    2. Developing a Strong Belief that You Can Do It. You can reach you goal.
    3. Hard Training. Strengthening the "I Can Do It" belief.

4. Visualization. Mentally achieving success prior to actual implementation.

5. Hard Training. Mental preparation is worthless without physical preparation. It has to hurt more than any race will ever hurt.

6. Race Planning. You need contingencies in case unforeseen problems arise.

7. Race Day Implementation. Implementation is the real test.

"A personal example in which I used the above techniques is my 1996 season. I set my goals which were two part: To achieve the Olympic Games B-Standard (this would require a 3 minute 21 second improvement of my 20km best), and to win the Olympic Trials 20km, thus doing all I could do to make the Olympic Team. In order to achieve goal two, goal one first had to be accomplished. So I broke my season into two parts so that I could focus on one goal at a time. Singular purpose in training helped me to achieve both goals in 1996.

"Fine, I had my goals, but were they realistic? Could I really drop over three minutes off my personal best? I wasn't 100% sure if I could, but I believed it was possible. Some of my friends in the sport told me I couldn't expect to make such improvements; told me I couldn't do it, no way, no how. I ignored them. I told myself I could do it and then I developed a training plan that helped me strengthen this belief. I broke the race down into pieces: 20 x 1km—all I had to do was drop around 10 seconds per kilometer and I would be there. So workouts included one kilometer repeats at goal pace with short rests (easy) and also some of the mental toughness builders like the two-hour+ treadmill sessions. Accomplishing the workouts helped build the belief that a sub-1:26 20km was possible. In fact the workouts were tough enough that they hurt worse than any race has ever hurt. I knew that if I was going to make a break through I had to be ready to tolerate some pain so I made sure I did so regularly in training.

"Race planning for my first goal—a sub-1:26 20km—was easy: even pace at around 1:25-1:26 pace the entire race, focusing on 1km at a time. Nothing more than a time trial with no need to worry about winning. Fortunately, I achieved the goal on the first try at the end of March and had several months to focus on Goal #2: winning the trials.

"Winning a race requires you to respond not only to your own body and feelings but to the actions of others. Thus mental preparation is even more important. Again, I structured workouts that focused on winning the trials. These included interval sessions in 90+ degree heat, a field trip to the race course with several training sessions on the course, and time trials to simulate race strategy.

"In addition to hard training, I began to visualize winning. With the course in mind, I played through various race scenarios and developed strategies on how to deal with them. I had a race plan and numerous contingency plans developed so that I was prepared mentally to deal with almost any situation. I went into the trials physically ready and mentally ready to win. The hard training made the trials race seem physically easy—I had done faster workouts in worse conditions on the same course. However, I believe the solid mental preparation was likely the key to my winning. I believed I could and would win and was thoroughly prepared to implement my race plan (or contingency plan) in order to win.

"In a nutshell my mental toughness derives mainly from my hard training, which helps me to solidify the belief that my goals will be accomplished. Various resources on sport psychology may be helpful for you in developing a mental preparation game plan. I'd refer you to one of the many sports psychology books and articles for a review of the subject and possible techniques that can be utilized. (*Sporting Body, Sporting Minds* is one I've consulted). Some of the techniques, such as visualization, found in the texts may be helpful to you. While you may disagree or find other suggestions totally useless.

"Regardless, after reading a psychology book or article, it's still up to you to implement and use the techniques effectively. At one Olympic Training Center camp for national racewalk team members, a sport psychologist noted that, as a group, the biggest mental challenge for the athletes appeared to be getting out the door to train every day rather than the mental aspects of racing. Thus most of the athletes were wasting their time focusing on mental race visualization, etc., because they were essentially unprepared to race due to day-to-day lapses in focus. You can visualize all day about winning the race, but it won't do you a bit of good unless you're prepared for the pain and physical stress that it will take to win. You still have to train and train hard."

Chapter 18: Visualization

Visualization is one of the most important psychological tools at any athlete's disposal—especially for athletes involved in technique intensive sports like racewalking. It's the act of programming your brain for the things that you *want* to occur in the future by playing a positive virtual reality "movie" over and over again in your head.

The brain is where the neuromuscular signals that control your walking begin. It's also where pain messages are processed. Visualization works because you can trick your brain into believing something that isn't true—*yet*. If you constantly play the right messages over and over again in your head, you can help bring about that fast, efficient, legal racewalking future. Visualization can't replace hard racewalking training, but it can be very effective as a shortcut to learning efficient technique, as a confidence builder, and as a relaxation technique.

Skill Learning

Technique improvements are most easily ingrained when you can first watch a model in person or on videotape. Then, by replaying in your mind the technique you've watched, your body will learn to make the adjustments.

If you don't have a good racewalking role model in your town, watch tapes of top walkers that you would like to emulate. Pick an athlete with a similar body type, and in your mind, play your own tape of you walking inside that person's body. Years ago, when trying to learn a more effective hip drive, I would often visualize my head on Carlos Mercenario's body. I would see my face, but the movements in my visualization were his. I would then imitate the actions while walking, still imagining Carlos' movements that I had seen in the video. After a while the actions felt comfortable and are now a part of my "natural" technique—I don't have to think about it any more while training or racing.

Even today, when I want to work on a different element of my technique, I'll pick a good role model and do the same thing. Try it, you'll be amazed!

92

From Dreams to Reality

Visualization can be a very important pre-competition confidence builder. Try to do your last workout before any important competition on the race course itself so you know the layout. By knowing the course you'll be able to create a mental image of yourself the night before the race; an image of you walking fast, efficiently and legally on the course during the next morning's race. Go over the tough parts of the course: the hills, the turns, etc., and focus on staying focused during these segments.

Ask yourself what you want to occur during the race, then make it happen in your mind. You must first be able to see yourself winning or walking that big personal record or you'll never accomplish your goals in reality. The next morning, bring your "dreams" to life: Wake up and make your visualized scenario happen.

Relaxation

Visualization can also be used as an excellent relaxation technique. If you feel yourself getting uptight before a race, tune out and take yourself away. Put yourself somewhere else, in a place where there are no worries. Perhaps you'd rather be at the beach or in a forest. Making sure you have a friend or an alarm set to rouse you in case you drift off *too* deeply, find a quiet spot away from your competitors and other distractions. Sit, or perhaps lay down under a tree, then think about that favorite beach or forest. Involve all your senses: See and hear the waves. Feel the warm sand on your feet and the sun on you face; or listen to the cascading waterfall and smell the trees in the forest.

While you're taking yourself away, focus on your heart rate. Breathe deeply and slowly, attempting to bring your pulse rate down. You'll have plenty of time to get your heart rate back up during your warm up, but use your pre-warm up visualization session to calm and fully relax yourself. Chapter 19 will further explain pre- and mid-competition relaxation techniques.

Bad Visuals

Visualization can be an extremely effective tool for breaking bad habits and learning good racewalking technique—it can also really screw you up if you're modeling your technique on a bad visual analogy. Here are a few common ones that can really mess you up:

1. Pull a rope. This is supposed to develop an effective arm swing. I know instantly when a group has been "infected" by this one: I'm confronted with 20 racewalking mimes pulling a dang imaginary rope. And I <u>hate</u> mimes! Forget the stupid rope. Just bend your elbows at 90 degrees, keep your shoulders relaxed and let the arms swing naturally, with a low and powerful arm stroke.

2. Pinch a coin. I'm just baffled by this one. How pinching a real or imaginary gold coin between your butt cheeks is going to make you walk faster is beyond my comprehension. If you need to imagine a gold coin, imagine it's at the finish line waiting for you—if you win. And if you feel the need to "pinch" your muscles, tighten your lower abdominals to facilitate a "tall" posture.

3. Prance like a horse. Horses are very fast, graceful animals—when they're running. When they're prancing *à la* dressage horses, everything is moving up and down and they're not moving forward very quickly at all. So if you want to racewalk slowly *and* lift, by all means, prance like a horse. When I think of a racewalking animal, I think of Carlos Mercenario, not some prancing pony.

4. Be a ski jumper. First of all, you shouldn't be trying to lean forward while you walk— this may be heretical to some, but you should *not* "put your nose over your toes." And besides, wrong sport, wrong season. You're *not* a ski jumper, you're a *racewalker,* so why not just imagine you're a racewalker?

Chapter 19: Relaxation

One of the keys to athletic success is the ability to relax both before and during competition. It's okay to be a little keyed up before a big race, but it can be very damaging to be an out of control bag of nerves. Nervous tension can lead to physical tension, embodied as tightness in the neck and shoulders. This tightness can in turn be conveyed to the hips, considerably decreasing effective stride length. Nervousness also stimulates the production of adrenaline which raises heart rate, leading to a decreased lactate threshold racing speed (LTRS).

These and other physical manifestations of nervousness are what cause many athletes to "choke" in high-pressure situations. If you lie awake in a cold sweat the night before races, if your heart rate is 130 before the gun even goes off, or if your race times don't seem to be indicative of your true level of fitness, this chapter is for you.

Self-Confidence

Self-confidence is the key to relaxation. You have to believe in yourself and constantly reinforce that belief to remain relaxed. If you still have worries before a race, write them down and look at your list rationally. What do you have control over? If you can't control it don't bother thinking about it. If you do have some control over your problem, take steps to remedy the situation. If you're thinking, "Wow, I'm really dehydrated," then drink! If you're saying, "I feel really tight," then stretch!

When you can't control something, frame your thoughts about it in the positive: The glass isn't half empty, it "runneth over." Your competitors will be worried that the race course has a lot of hills, but you'll be thinking there are as many downhill sections as uphill sections. If your arch-rival shows up at a race unexpectedly you should be thinking, "Great! Now I have some good competition to pull me along."

And as far as that arch-rival goes, it doesn't hurt to "talk trash" (to yourself) a little to get your confidence up. Be friendly, smile, shake hands with your competitors, then after they leave tell them how badly you're going to kick their butts. Be as smug or "catty" as you need to be, as long as you're only talking to yourself: "Nice new shoes, Joe. Too bad they'll be finishing five minutes behind my old K-Mart specials...."

Distraction Control

You have enough psychological baggage to worry about when racing without getting hung up on *externalities*. Try to concern yourself only with the things you have some reasonable control over—your body and mind—don't get flustered by anything that's beyond your control. If it's hot and humid, it's hot and humid for everybody. The person who's going to be affected the most is the person who's getting his blood pressure up worrying that it's hot and humid. If there's nothing you can do about it, don't waste your energy complaining.

Whenever you feel these negative thoughts creeping in, talk them back to get yourself back on track. Learn to practice *distraction control*. It's okay to rationalize or lie to yourself if you have to: "It's not *really* hot out here. It'll get a lot better once the gun goes off." The only things worth thinking about are the things you can control. You can't control the weather or your competitors, but you can control how you react to them.

Back in the '80s there was a racewalker who would somehow always be around while I was warming up before races with some of the other athletes. Within 30 seconds of latching on to our group, he would start filing his excuses: "I can't believe I'm even here. I *tore* my hamstring during practice on Tuesday... Man, my back is killing me. I think I have a herniated disk... My glands sure are swollen. Are your glands swollen? I think I have that flu that's been going around...." Within 5 minutes of listening to this walking ball of negative energy we would all feel completely sapped; infected with contagious hypochondria. Before long we'd be saying things like, "You know, my back kind of hurts too," or "I don't feel very good either. Maybe I'll just do this race as a workout—even if it *is* the national championship..."

If you run into one of these Negative Nellies—and you will—don't even bother with distraction control techniques. There's no way you'll be able to talk yourself down from a prolonged contact with one of these black holes of negative energy. Don't allow yourself to get sucked into the void—get away as quickly as possible. Duck into the nearest Port-A-Potty if you have to, but get away. Negative energy is extremely contagious and it will affect your race if you let it.

A simple radio or tape player with headphones can be a very effective distraction-control device. If you need to tune out, *tune in* to your favorite station or put on your favorite tape to block out negative influences, and to help you to focus on your own thoughts.

Staying Calm During Judged Races

Finally, about those judges—the people we love to hate: They're your friends! They're out there on the course to make sure *the other guy* isn't cheating! But just in case a judge decides to give *you* a "friendly advice" caution paddle, simply acknowledge it, then concentrate on your race. Just trust your technique and relax! You've done your technique work, the drills, the economy intervals, so have confidence in your technique.

Don't let the judges or anybody else rattle you. Block them out of your mind and keep hammering. If you think too much about the judges you'll wind up changing your technique when you go by them and risk doing something you're not used to; something that's probably illegal.

Although "common sense" may tell you otherwise, you shouldn't necessarily slow down if you get a caution. It's actually counterproductive to do so: The slower your turnover, the easier it is for a judge to see what your feet or knees are doing. You may also wind up walking with a longer stride that will keep you off the ground even longer and make it more difficult to straighten your knees.

Remember to always frame things in the positive: A caution means you're doing great—you're at the very upper end of fast, legal technique. An actual "red card," now called a warning, isn't a good thing, but even collecting two red cards can be looked at as a technically perfect race: borderline but not out. You've pushed the limits of fast, legal technique without going overboard. Whatever happens, smile! What kind of cretin would give a disqualification to a relaxed, smiling athlete?

Just When You Thought You'd Seen it All...

Despite hernia surgery and a hepatitis attack just before the '92 Olympic Trials, I was in great shape, but disappointed at not making The Team. I decided to race a 20km three weeks later at New York's Empire State Games in Albany, hoping to hit a fast time to prove my fitness. It was a cool, rainy day—great weather compared to the horrible conditions at the trials. The course had several tight, single-cone turn-arounds, including one just a few feet before a curb that dropped off into a parking lot, but it was still relatively flat and fast. Approaching this turn on my second lap of the 2km course I saw a small boy sitting behind the cone with an umbrella, entirely blocking the turn. I shouted a few times but he didn't hear me so I continued on, not wanting to startle him. Just as I was about to go around him he heard me and jumped up in exactly the wrong spot. I was proud of the way I handled it, putting my hand on his shoulder and pivoting around without knocking him over or falling off the curb.

I didn't think another thing about it, and went on to hit splits of 21:30, 43:27, 1:05:12—on pace for my first sub-1:27:00 20km, and feeling great. With 400 meters to go and the finish line in sight I was confronted by a police car coming towards me right on the course. I moved closer to the water tables to get out of the way, but it kept coming at me. When the car was about 30 meters away the driver pulled a Starsky & Hutch, braking and sharply cutting the wheel so the car turned sideways and stopped directly in front of me. I tried to squeeze past but the Bozo threw open his door, hitting me in the hip. "Officer Prendergast" grabbed me by the arm, threw me against the car and slammed my chin against the roof. He kept yelling, asking me if I knew what "this" was all about and demanding identification—keep in mind I had identification numbers pinned to my front and back.... Super Cop finally fumed, "*Nobody* roughs little kids up on my beat," which finally gave me my first clue what was happening.

Before long every judge, volunteer and spectator within a half mile came running over to find out why I was about to be handcuffed. I was permitted to finish—in 1:28:45, 9 seconds *slower* than my PR—after race officials promised I wouldn't go anywhere afterwards. Within minutes I was led away and taken to the police station. The father, who apparently misunderstood his four-year-old son's description of the event and thought someone was trying to abduct the kid, never showed up to press charges so I got off with a warning. Prendergast didn't get off so easy; I went to the press room and told every newspaper in New York what happened. Even the New York Times picked it up. I'm still trying to figure out the moral of the story, but there's probably some great sports psychology message in there somewhere....

Chapter 20: Associative Thinking

Successful athletes are *associative*—they are at all times aware of their bodies and their environment when competing. You need to be alert, maintaining intense focus during the competition. Don't race dissociatively, on "cruise control." It's easy to let the pace fall off or to let other athletes pull away from you when the going gets tough if you're not focused on your body and the race going on around you.

You need to remain focused to keep your turnover rate up despite fatigue or pain, and you can't do that if you're off in space somewhere thinking about unicorns, hoping that it will make the pain go away. Racing is supposed to be difficult, but the pain is temporary. The gnawing afterthoughts of racing poorly in a big competition, however, can stay with you forever!

Body Check

Challenge the negatives. If you're feeling pain, don't deny it, use it: "My legs are burning, but that means I'm working hard. I can handle more. Now I've got to maintain my turnover and keep hitting the splits." If you are pushing too hard, be aware of the situation. If you're laboring in the first few minutes of the race, don't keep hammering away only to blow up in the second half of the race; ease up a little.

At key points in the race make a full body technique check—"How are my shoulders?" "Good—nice and relaxed." "How are the legs feeling?" "Just great, Dave. Really solid, and turning over quickly." "Lungs?" "No problem. Breathing's under control—I've got this thing sewn up!"

Watch Your Competitors

In addition to monitoring your own effort, it's also a good idea to occasionally try to gauge how your competitors are feeling. If someone you're racing looks like he's hurting, pick up the pace for a few minutes to break him. Try to make sure your own face is relaxed, though. It'll help keep you loose, and your competitor will think you're feeling much better than he is. You'd be surprised how many walkers will settle for second place when you speed past them, looking strong and relaxed while they are hurting or simply not focusing on staying competitive.

Keep Your Eye on the Ball

Above all, use your mind to your advantage—don't let it use you. On a base level, there's no life-or-death reason to want to racewalk fast. (Believe it or not, most people *run* away from bears, they don't racewalk.) Since racewalking isn't high on Abraham Maslow's hierarchy of human needs, you sometimes have to trick your mind into thinking that it really is a worthwhile pursuit—especially when it involves subjecting your body to the physical and psychological stresses of racing. To do so you must be able to focus on your body and how it is performing during the race.

When the going gets tough, zero in on maintaining a high stride rate and staying relaxed, and remind yourself why you're doing this: If your goal is to win the race, remind yourself of that goal if somebody passes you in the final stages of the race. If you let him go because you're hurting, you're not going to win. If your goal is a time goal, on the other hand, watch the clock. Keep track of your splits, and force yourself to spin the wheels a little quicker if you start falling off the pace.

Final Thoughts

You know how to train now—you're the coach and you're in control of your own racewalking destiny. Set ambitious but reasonable goals for yourself, make a plan to achieve them, visualize your goals becoming reality, then stick to your plan and make it so. Let each small victory motivate you to raise the bar a bit higher, then visualize yourself achieving the next success. If you can't imagine racewalking fast and with perfect technique, and if you don't believe you can beat your rivals and your best times, you're probably right.

During competitions, stay alert and in control of your mind. Challenge the negative thoughts with positives at all cost. Your brain *will* try to make you slow down when things start to hurt. Be ready for it, and don't let it happen. There are always two feuding influences in your head during competitions: the one that wants to be a champion, and the one that wants to go home and take a nap. It's up to you to decide which will come out on top.

Finally, after races, evaluate and write down in your training log what went right or wrong. Keep track of anything you did that seemed to help your race, as well as anything you may have done wrong that may have hurt it. If you don't know your own history, you're doomed to repeating your mistakes, and failing to replicate your successes.

Tim Seaman on:

Staying Motivated by Being Part of a Team

Accomplishments: 2000 Olympian, Olympic Trials Champion and Olympic Trials record-holder at 20 kilometers. American record-holder at 3K, 5K, 10K and 20K.

Personal Records:
1 mile:	5:51
3 kilometers:	11:19
5 kilometers:	19:09
10 kilometers:	39:23
20 kilometers:	1:23:40

Background: Tim, originally from Long Island, New York, started racewalking in the 11th grade. He started as a runner, but began entering the 1-mile walk to score points for the track team. Tim's rapid improvement in the walk earned him a scholarship to compete for the University of Wisconsin-Parkside where he became the only four-time NAIA Outdoor National Champion in the history of the school. After graduating in 1995, Tim moved to LaGrange, GA to train with other Olympic hopefuls. He thrived in the team environment in LaGrange, walking 1:24:14 for 20km and placing 2nd at the 1996 Olympic Trials. After 1996 Tim moved to the U.S. Olympic Training Center in Chula Vista, California where he continues to train with Curt Clausen, John Nunn, Olympic Champion Jefferson Perez, and other elite racewalkers.

Tim says: "All throughout high school, I played soccer in the fall and then ran indoor and outdoor track. So I had a deeply rooted "team-player" mindset before I even started racewalking. I actually began racewalking to earn points for the team. Then, at Parkside, I was very proud to win four NAIA racewalk championships to help out my team, and now, as a member of the New York Athletic Club, I help the club in the Indoor and Outdoor Nationals team standings when I place in these events. When I race, I race for myself, but it's always a great motivator for me to know that I'm helping out my team as well.

"Throughout high school and college, in LaGrange, and now here in Chula Vista, I've always trained as part of a group. I've really enjoyed the camaraderie that comes from working out with so many great training partners over the years. Without their support, I don't know if I would have stayed with racewalking as long as I have. Even when we race, we try to help each other out if we can, sharing the pacing responsibilities or helping each other to pull away from other walkers. I'll always remember competing in a 20km race in Bekescsaba, Hungary with Dave in 1996. I had never walked under 1:29 before, but by walking together, and helping each other through the rough spots, we were both able to walk under 1:25. It was a great thrill to make such a big improvement, but it was even more special to be able to share the experience with one of my training partners who also had a great race.

"I've always trained hard as a racewalker, but I try to never let it get in the way of me having fun. The key to training and racing well is really to have fun with what you are doing. If you are not having fun you will not do well. You and you alone must want to do this, and you and you alone will be the person who has to make most of the sacrifices. But sharing the good times, as well as the tough times, with other like-minded athletes really makes the tough workouts and races a lot easier to handle.

"Taking it easy and enjoying yourself is the only way to stay motivated in your training—and you should make sure that you're having fun when competing in races as well. Don't dread them: Take them as opportunities to test yourself, not as pressure-packed do-or-die situations."

SECTION IV: IT AIN'T JUST WALKIN'

OTHER STUFF YOU NEED TO DO TO ENSURE SUCCESS

It is often said that racewalkers *need* to do one thing or another, but walkers only *need* to get out the door and train more. There are, however, a lot of things that we really *should* be doing a lot more of. First are stretching and dynamic flexibility drills; next, abdominal work; then if you have time, swimming to loosen those tight racewalking muscles (and for excellent cardio-vascular cross-training); and finally, once you're doing everything else, you should be lifting weights.

Take it from this battered old dog: The older you get, the more you need to look at this ancillary stuff. The strength and flexibility benefits of weights, stretching, drills, etc., can *probably* make you faster on their own accord. But more importantly, they can keep you healthy and injury-free which will allow you to keep training consistently. And that will *definitely* make you a better walker.

Chapter 21: Stretching

Racewalking is first and foremost a technique event. Like any other technique-intensive sport or track and field event, it requires a full range of motion for optimal performance. Unfortunately, racewalking is also an endurance event which, like running, promotes tightness and inflexibility in the muscle groups used. Remember, you're being propelled forward by *contracting* muscles. Over time, these muscles incrementally lose flexibility if they're not stretched gently after exercise. If properly stretched, muscles are lengthened and circulation is enhanced. Increased flexibility enables a more fluid, efficient style that will allow you to walk much faster with reduced chance of injury.

Types of Stretches

There are three different types of stretching: ballistic or "bouncy" stretches, static stretches and proprioceptive neuromuscular facilitation (PNF) or "contract/release" stretches.

Ballistic stretches. Ballistic stretches are the old-fashioned military toe touches and the like. They can trigger a protective contraction in the muscle that defeats the purpose of stretching—to *loosen* the muscles. Ballistic stretches should not be used.

Static stretches. Static stretches are slow easy stretches that are held for at least 20-30 seconds. While stretching, breathe normally into the stretch—don't hold your breath. Mild tension should be felt in the muscle, not pain.

PNF Stretches. The third type of stretches, PNF exercises, are a way of tricking the neuromuscular system into allowing a deeper stretch than you would otherwise be able to achieve with ordinary static stretches. First the muscle to be stretched is contracted for 10-20 seconds, then allowed to relax for three to 10 seconds. Then you perform a static stretch for the usual 20-30 seconds. The process is repeated several times. Again, don't stretch to the point of pain or else muscle contraction and possible injury will result.

Tight Spots

Stretching is most effectively used to improve flexibility in an individual walker's own particular "tight spots." Each racewalker will have different problem areas, but a few notoriously tight muscle groups common to many walkers are:

1. Hamstrings

The hamstrings are the muscles on the back of the thigh. Tight, weak hamstrings can lead to knee-straightening problems, can limit stride, and can create an undesirable increase in your "flight phase." The hamstrings are also one of the most common chronic injury areas for racewalkers. To stretch the hamstrings, lie down on your back, then raise one leg and grab it with both hands behind the belly, or middle part, of the hamstring.

Keep the opposite leg bent and the abdominals tensed to maintain a "pelvic tilt." Tense the hamstrings for five seconds by pushing against your hands, then relax and stretch for 20 seconds. Repeat with the other leg.

The seated toe-touch is another great hamstring stretch. Sit with one leg bent in front of you and the other leg straight and out to the side. With your back flat, reach for the toes on the foot of the straightened leg. Hold for 20-30 seconds. If you can't reach the foot you can use a towel to assist.

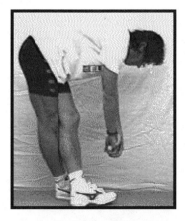

Finally, try the "passive hang" to stretch the upper part of the hamstrings and the lower back. Start with your feet together, about shoulder-width apart, then simply bend over at the waist and reach for your toes. Hold the position for about 20 seconds, then repeat with the right leg crossed in front of the left, then again with the left leg crossed in front of the right.

2. Groin/gracilis muscle

The gracilis originates in the groin area and inserts below the knee on the inside of the leg. It's another commonly injured muscle/tendon complex.

To stretch the gracilis, sit on the floor with the soles of the feet together. Press your elbows into your inner thighs to provide resistance, then contract for five seconds, attempting to bring the knees together against the resistance. Relax, then stretch by pushing your knees towards the floor for 20 seconds.

The wall straddle is another great gracilis stretch. First sit sideways against a wall, then turn yourself around 90 degrees so you're laying flat on your back with your legs straddling the wall. Let your legs drop until you feel a good stretch in the groin and along the inside of the thigh. As the muscle relaxes allow your feet to drop further down the wall. Hold for several minutes.

The "Asian squat" is a great all-around stretch, primarily for the groin, but also for the lower back and the calves. Simply squat straight down with your feet flat on the floor, arms hanging in front or holding your ankles for balance.

Finally, try a kneeling squat to really get the inner thigh. Simply kneel down, then extend one leg straight out to the side, then squat down, pressing the heel into the floor until you feel a good stretch all along the inner thigh.

3. Quadriceps

The quads are the muscles at the front of the thigh. Increased quadriceps flexibility will further enhance effective stride length and will allow easier knee straightening. Lie down on your right side, then grab the left ankle or the front of the shin with your left hand. Pull back to stretch the quad. You're not trying to get your heel to touch your butt, you're trying to pull the leg back away from the other. Repeat on the other side.

The quadriceps stretch can also be performed while standing, but be sure to hold onto a wall or other stable support with your free hand. Again, remember to pull the leg away from the other leg, rather than trying to bring your heel towards your butt which can put an undue strain on the knee.

4. Piriformis/iliotibial band

The piriformis and iliotibial band both originate in the buttocks and are both very common injury-prone areas for racewalkers. Flexibility in the piriformis/iliotibial band area will also help hip drop, ease knee-straightening and will allow a more efficient in-line foot plant. To stretch the I.T. band, sit with the right leg out in front of you, and the left leg bent at the knee with the left foot flat on the floor to the right of the right knee. "Hug" your left knee and pull it towards your chest until you feel a good stretch in the left buttock.

To stretch the piriformis and ease tightness in the iliotibial band, start out kneeling with both hands on the floor in front of you. Bring the right knee forward and out to the side so the right foot lies flat under your body, then extend the left leg back behind you so your weight is over the right foot. You should feel a stretch on the outside of the gluteus and along the iliotibial band. Hold for 20 seconds then repeat on the other side.

Another good stretch for the piriformis: Simply lay flat on your stomach with your knees bent at 90-degree angles. Allow your feet to drop outwards, towards the floor until you feel a good stretch on the outside of the hip, and in the sacro-iliac joint of the lower back. It looks easy, but you'll definitely feel it!

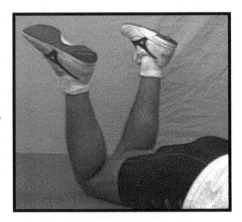

5. Lower back

Crippling lower back pain has been my downfall over the years, causing me to miss more workouts and races than any other injury. Since tight

hamstrings will "pull" at their insertion points in the pelvis, hamstring stretches will relieve some strain on the lower back. In addition, try the "brick," the "seal" and the "sen." For the brick, you'll need a brick or a book about two inches thick. Simply stand "at attention" with one foot on the brick, and the other foot flat on the floor, making sure that both knees remain straight. You should feel a good stretch right in the sacro-iliac joint, and in the gluteal muscles that lead into it.

To do the seal, simply lay flat on your stomach then do a push up, arching your back while keeping your belly flat on the floor. Hold for 20-30 seconds.

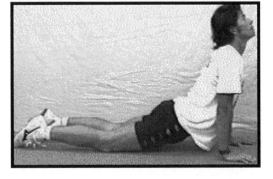

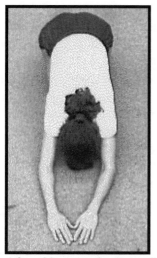

For the sen, kneel down on all fours with your arms stretched out in front of you and you palms on the floor, then sit back on your heels to stretch the lower back.

After 20 seconds, "crawl" with your hands as far as you can to the left, then to the right to stretch out the muscles leading into the sacroiliac joint. Take it slow, this one feels really good!

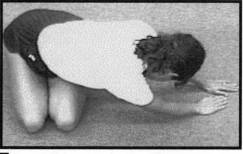

6. Shins

You don't really use your shin muscles except when racewalking, so they'll be sore for a while until you develop them. Massage them, then try the following: Sit "Indian style" with one leg crossed over the other. Dorsi-flex your ankle, bringing the top of your foot closer to your shin, while pushing down on the top of the foot with your hand to provide resistance. Hold for five seconds, then relax and stretch, pointing the toes and pulling down with the hand to stretch the shins. Change the angle of the foot slightly to get both the tibialis anterior muscles on the front of, and the peroneus muscles along the outside of the shin.

7. Hip flexors/iliopsoas

Flexible hip flexors will allow you to achieve an increased stride length behind your body. This provides a longer stride without sacrificing turnover rate, resulting in a more powerful push from the rear. Step forward with your left leg so your left foot is flat on the ground, and your knee is bent at 90 degrees so your thigh is parallel to the ground. To limit strain on the knee, keep it directly over the foot. Your right leg should be extended way back behind you. Now drop straight down to stretch the iliopsoas—the strongest hip flexor, which runs from the low back around to the front and into the lower abdominal region.

8. Calves

More supple calf muscles and increased range of motion in the ankle joint will allow greater rear-stride length and will enable a more powerful toe-off. To stretch the gastroc nemius and the soleus muscles of the calf, stand on your toes for about 10 seconds to contract the muscles.

Relax, then step way back with one foot to stretch the gastroc nemius muscle in the upper part of the calf. Hold for about 20 seconds. To get the soleus muscle in the lower part of the calf, bend the knee for 20 seconds, keeping the foot flat on the ground.

9. Behind your knees

Is there a name for the back of your knees? Whatever they're called, this is a common sore spot, especially for beginning racewalkers, since many of the calf, hamstring and quadriceps muscles originate or insert here. To stretch the backs of the knees, the calves and hamstrings all at once, stand with the front of one foot up on a curb, brick or 2 x 4, then, keeping your knees straight, simply bend down to touch your toes. Hold for 20 seconds.

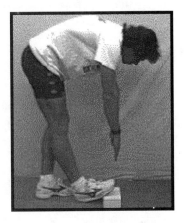

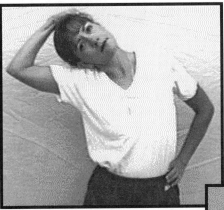

10. Neck and shoulders

Upper-body relaxation is one of the most important elements of a smooth, efficient walking technique. Tension in the upper body will be transferred to the hips; stride length will be reduced and you'll be more prone to an increase in the "vertical component of the

reaction forces,"—in other words, lifting. For a PNF stretch, push your head sideways against your hand for five seconds, then let it drop to the other side. Pull it gently towards your shoulder for 20 seconds to stretch the neck and trapezius muscles. To stretch the entire shoulder area, hold your right arm parallel to the ground with the elbow bent at 90 degrees. Push out against your hand for five seconds to contract the sub-scapular muscles, then stretch them by bringing the upper arm towards your chest by pulling from the elbow with your free hand. As always, hold for 20 seconds.

11. Chest/pectoralis major

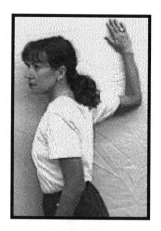

Face a wall with your elbow bent at 90 degrees and your forearm vertical—like you're waving to the wall. Push against the wall with the palm of your hand, your forearm and your biceps for five seconds, then relax. Keeping your arm flat against the wall, turn your body sideways, using the wall to stretch the chest and shoulder muscles. You can also do the same stretch with your fist against the wall and your arm fully extended to stretch the upper arm and shoulder.

Before or After?

Of course there are many more stretches than the few I've described here, but these are a good starting point. By doing the stretches in the order presented you can begin on the floor, then work up to the standing stretches before "hitting the showers." You may want to do some kind of stretching before training to make the workout feel good, but since stretching "cold" muscles can lead to injuries, dynamic flexibility drills, discussed in the next chapter, are generally better than static stretches for pre-workout stretching. Long-term gains in flexibility will come from stretching warm muscles *after* your workouts.

It's a good idea to spend a good 10-15 minutes stretching all the major muscle groups after every workout—especially after the long or fast sessions. You should also try to spend at least 1/2 hour about three times per week on a more comprehensive stretching program for increased range of motion and injury prevention.

For more stretches, there are dozens of excellent books on stretching. Bob Anderson's *Stretching* is the best known, but you need to find the particular stretches that work for you, so shop around. Also, experiment to see which positions get it right where it hurts.

Basic Stretching Principles

- Warm up first to increase circulation before stretching.

- Stretch gently—stop if it hurts.

- Focus on the muscle being stretched.

- Breathe rhythmically.

- Stretch the tighter side first.

- After stretching one group of muscles, stretch the antagonist group—i.e., stretch the quadriceps, then the hamstrings.

- For PNF stretches, tense for 5-10 seconds, relax for three to five seconds then stretch for 20 seconds.

- Maintain good posture at all times.

Self Massage

While stretching, feel around for "knots" in your muscles. These knots of "necrotic tissue" are actually damaged muscle fibers. These knots have the same effect on your muscles as knots in a piece of rope or string: The muscle gets "bunched up" at the damaged spots and is incrementally shortened. By working out the knots with cross-fiber strokes with your fingers, you can help to lengthen and loosen the muscles. Using a small wooden or plastic massage tool will save your fingers from fatigue, and a Thera-cane—a long, curved heavy-duty plastic stick with round knobs at either end—will help you to reach spots you just can't get with your fingers.

Chapter 22: Dynamic Flexibility Drills

Although the stretching exercises described in chapter 21 are very important for increasing *static* flexibility, they're only part of the story. These static exercises can certainly help to develop long-term gains in flexibility, but they give better results when used *after* training. Since racewalking is a *dynamic* activity, static stretches done before workouts are of limited value in preparing the body to racewalk. You need to do *dynamic flexibility drills* before training to fully prepare your body to walk—for the sake of your technique, and to prevent injuries.

Have you ever seen an Olympic gymnast running up to the vault? They're among the most flexible athletes on the planet, yet most gymnasts run extremely awkwardly. Too much static flexibility can actually be detrimental to a racewalker because you wind up having to contract the muscles to artificially limit their range of motion. For example, you have to force a contraction to get the heel down quickly instead of allowing the natural elasticity of the hamstring muscles to do it for you.

Gains in static flexibility increase the range of motion of resting muscles and may help prevent injuries, but racewalkers must also do dynamic flexibility drills to increase flexibility throughout the dynamic range of the racewalking motion. Dynamic flexibility drills can also be used as technique drills to help develop racewalking-specific neuromuscular coordination.

Specific Drills

The following drills should be used as part of your daily warm-up routine—especially on speed work and competition days. Always start slowly. Work up from a few repetitions at first to 15-20 repetitions, and gradually increase the range of motion from one repetition to the next until full extension is reached over the last few repeats. Always maintain good posture when doing drills, and don't overdo it; work the muscles through a sufficient range of motion to allow a good stretch, but don't work to the point of pain—drills are part of your warm-up, not a competitive activity.

1. Leg Swings. Stand sideways next to a wall or fence, steadying yourself by holding on to it with one hand. Swing your outside leg front to back, bending the knee as it comes forward, straightening as it goes back. Accentuate the back portion of the swing to stretch the hamstring, gluteus and lower back muscles. Do 15-20 swings, then turn around and repeat with the other leg. Swinging the free arm the opposite direction of the leg will help develop bilateral coordination.

2. Side Swings. Stand about two feet from the wall with your feet about shoulder-width apart. Holding on to the wall with both hands, swing your right leg to the outside, then to the inside about 12-20 times to stretch the groin and outside of the hip. Repeat with the left leg about 12-20 times.

3. Swedish Twists. Grab that wall again, standing about 2 feet away. Tuck your right foot behind your left knee, then swing the right knee towards the wall, then back, keeping the foot tucked behind the knee. Repeat 12-20 times, then repeat with the other leg. Great for the lower

 back and groin. Most drills are pretty universal, but I've only seen this drill done in Sweden.

4. Hip Wangers. Again, hold on to the wall with both hands, and feet about shoulder-width apart. Keeping your arms outstretched, lean into

the wall with your pelvis, then circumscribe a large circle with the hips to stretch the entire pelvic area. Do 8 to 10 circles clockwise, then 8 to 10 circles counter-clockwise. Named in honor of Mel McGinnis, a former 50km National Team member who became a minister in 1986. Mel performed a version of the Wanger during a sermon at the 1986 Olympic Festival to graphically illustrate the evils of "Wild" dancing and other forms of National Team debauchery.

5. Rock & Roll. Stand sideways to the wall. Balance on your heels with one foot about 24" in front of the other. Throw your pelvis forward, rolling up onto the toes of both feet. Rock back onto your heels, then repeat, rocking back and forth 12-15 times. Put your other foot forward, then rock and roll again about 12-15 more times.

6. Knee Pumps. Again, hold onto the wall, with feet together about four feet from the wall. Stand on the balls of your feet without bending at the waist. Pump each knee forward quickly, rolling up onto the toes of the pumping foot. Pump each leg 12-20 times.

7. Hurdler's Drill. Standing about three feet from the wall, lift one leg out to the side with the knee bent, as if over an imaginary hurdle. "Hurdle" five times with each leg. The hurdler's drill is a great warm-up for the groin and hip-flexors.

8. Arm Swings. With your palms facing outward and your elbows straight, "backstroke" with each arm, holding the shoulder close to the

ear. Do 12-20 swings with each arm for upper body flexibility. Swinging both arms at the same time, 180 degrees apart, helps to develop coordination.

9. Torso Twists. Stand with your feet shoulder-width apart, arms outstretched and parallel to the ground. Keeping the feet planted, twist the torso fully by swinging the arms to the left, then to the right. Repeat 12-20 times. Torso twists are great for loosening up the lower back and shoulders.

10. Toe Touches. Take a small step forward with your right foot. With the right leg straight, gently bend down and touch your toes, then stand up straight to stretch the lower back. Now step forward with the left leg.

Gently bend down and touch your toes again. Repeat five to ten times on each side.

11. Long Arms. Racewalk slowly with your arms straight and your palms facing back. Push off the tips of the toes to accentuate the back part of your stride. The long arms drill helps to teach proper toe push-off, opens up the hips and stretches the groin.

12. Quick Steps. Self explanatory. Walk with an extremely short stride, one heel landing almost on top of the toes of the other foot. Take very

quick steps. Quick steps teach quick turnover, reinforce a short stride in front of the body, and help to teach proper knee-straightening.

13. Figure Eights.
Walk quickly, with very short strides in a tight figure-eight pattern. The figure-eight drill helps to develop quick turnover, a feel for landing along

the outside part of the sole of the foot, and teaches you tight-turning ability for those single-cone turn-around courses.

14. The Twist. Standing with feet shoulder-width apart, twist your torso fully to the left. Now jump up, twisting your torso fully to the right, and the feet to the left. Repeat quickly 10-12 times. The lower body should twist counter-clockwise as the upper body twists clockwise and *vice versa.* Great for the lower back, and for developing hip rotation and lower-leg strength.

After your warm up and drills, do a few accelerations before the start of the workout or race. Start out by walking at an easy pace, then accelerate smoothly to top speed by 25 meters. Hold top speed for approximately 20 meters, then decelerate. Spending 5 or 10 minutes doing dynamic flexibility drills and accelerations before each workout will give you better range of motion for your workout, and will help you to develop lasting racewalking-specific coordination.

Andrzej Chylinski on:
Technique and Flexibility Drills

Accomplishments: 1996 Olympian at 50 kilometers. 1993, '95, and '97 World Cup Team member. 1992, '94 and '96 Pan Am Cup Team member.

Personal Records:
5 kilometers: 19:50
10 kilometers: 41:50
20 kilometers: 1:26:23
50 kilometers: 3:58:39

Background: Andrzej was born in New York City in 1960, but moved to Warsaw, Poland at the age of two. Holding a U.S. passport, and wanting to make the 1991 U.S. World Cup Team, Andrzej flew from Poland to the trial race in San Jose, California, arriving only hours before the competition. He finished 8th, but was 4th at the National 20km two months later in New York City—his "hometown." Andrzej settled in Colorado Springs, Colorado, leaving behind his job as a journalist in Warsaw, to work as a dishwasher at the U.S. Olympic Training Center—a sacrifice but, he says, a necessary one that afforded him the training time he needed to reach his ultimate goal: A spot on the 1992 U.S. Olympic Team.

Before long, Andrzej rose to the upper echelon of the U.S. walking ranks. He made several U.S. international teams, but failed to make the Olympic Team in 1992. Undaunted, he continued on, finally fulfilling his dream by walking 3:58:39 for 50km to earn a spot on the 1996 team.

Learning to racewalk in eastern Europe, Andrzej had the importance of dynamic flexibility exercises "drilled" into him from his earliest days as a racewalker. As long as I've known him, he has done an extraordinary variety of drills before every workout or competition.

Andrzej Says: "I believe that dynamic flexibility drills are one of the most important things a racewalker can do to improve his abilities. I do some static stretching now, as well, but before moving to the U.S. in 1991 I had never even heard of these "sitting" stretches.

"Before every workout in Poland we always jogged one or two kilometers, then racewalked slowly doing a number of upper-body flexibility drills while walking, followed by about 10 minutes of racewalking-specific drills. I still follow the same 30-minute routine before every workout or competition.

"Carl Schueler introduced me to static stretching when I moved to Colorado. I do about 10-15 minutes of these stretches after the workout for injury prevention, but I never stretch cold muscles before training.

"I race 50kms frequently [Andrzej walked eleven 50s between February, 1995 and April, 1997] and I'm not so young anymore, so flexibility drills are even more important for me now. But I believe that every walker of any age or ability level should do these exercises every day."

Chapter 23: Strength Training

Racewalking does a lot of things for you, but it does not build muscular strength. Despite all the great enzymatic changes you'll get from distance work, the muscles themselves may actually get weaker since distance work increases the percentage of oxidative-glycolytic (endurance) muscle fibers and decreases the percentage of fast glycolytic (strength/speed) fibers. Weaker muscles are more injury prone, and less able to maintain high stride rates for the duration of long races. In addition to improving overall strength, weight training can also help your technique and speed.

The Variables

The variables in any weight-training program are: intensity (the percentage of your maximum lifting ability that you lift during a particular exercise), number of repetitions, and duration of the workout. The variables will change depending on what your goals are. There are two basic approaches:

Lifting for Strength. Lift heavy weights with few (about 8-10) repetitions to build explosive strength.

Lifting for Endurance. Lift at about 70% of maximum and do more repeats (about 15-20) to build endurance.

Racewalking is a lot like sprinting: Both are "explosive" activities, requiring a high number of repeats (strides) per second. We need to maximize turnover rate, and that requires muscular strength. Lifting fewer repetitions with heavy weights will build this maximal strength. Long rests between sets will enable you to lift heavier weights.

Having said that, we're also out there for a whole lot longer than a 10-second sprint. We need to lift for endurance as well. The traditional runners' approach is to do two or three sets of 20 RM lifts. (RM = repetitions maximum. One RM is the amount of weight that you're are able to lift one time, but not two. 10 RM is the amount of weight that you're able to lift ten times before failure.) But 20 repetitions is not real endurance. Since we're moving our arms and legs somewhere in the neighborhood of 200 times per minute, lifting a light weight 20 times is not going to build sufficient muscular endurance.

Some elite walkers believe that to make real gains in endurance, your weight workouts should approach race duration. 20km walkers should lift for 1:20-1:30. That's a LOT of sets! For example, four to six sets of 15-20 repetitions of each exercise with short—less than one minute—rests between sets. I believe that if you have that much time to train your efforts will be rewarded more by spending more time walking and stretching instead of spending half the day in the weight room.

Specificity

Resistance applied to the limbs during actual phases of the racewalking stride or arm swing are the most specific strengthening possible. Racewalking on hills provides this type of resistance, and is perhaps the most racewalking-specific resistance training there is. Hill training should be incorporated into any racewalker's schedule—especially during base-building periods.

Specificity should also be your goal in the weight room. Whether you decide to lift heavy weights, lighter weights or both, racewalking-specific exercises should be employed. Nautilus or other machines should be chosen carefully to work primarily those muscles and ranges of motion that will actually be used while racewalking.

If you can't find machines to mimic the action, use free weights or elastic devices. Very specific exercises can be developed using a "Theraband" or other elastic devices, like surgical tubing or a slit bicycle tube, for example. Simply anchor one end of the band to piece of furniture or door knob, then loop the other end around your foot or hand and perform arm or leg swings to strengthen the muscles used while racewalking. Although they are of limited value in strength-building, arm swings using light (three to five pound) free weights while standing in front of a mirror are excellent walking-specific exercises that will help to develop upper body coordination.

Consistency

When starting a weight-training program you should think long-term. Real strength gains take time. You'll probably greatly improve your lifting ability in the first few weeks of your training program, but this improved ability is simply improved coordination, as opposed to "real" strength gains. You need to make cellular changes after these neurological "learning" changes. Once made, these strength gains can be lost surprisingly quickly, especially if you're walking a lot of miles, so you need to consistently do two to three sessions per week.

Controlled Explosions

According to Steve Fleck, director of the strength training facility at the US Olympic Training Center in Colorado Springs, you should control the weights, lifting as quickly as possible without using momentum. Although many trainers recommend lifting for a count of two then lowering the weight for a count of four, Fleck says: "You don't get results from going slow, you must lift explosively." Fleck recommends both lifting and lowering for counts of two.

Fleck also recommends working the large muscle groups first, then the smaller ones. Start with relatively heavy weights and lower repetitions on the legs, abdomen and lower back, then move on to higher repetitions with lighter weights for the arms.

Absolutely Work Your "Abs"

Even if you do no other resistance training, you should take the time to work your abdominal muscles. The hip and upper leg area is the "engine" for the competitive racewalker and strong abdominals are a vital component. The abs provide a stable support for many of the large lower-body muscles, so strengthening them will reduce strain on the hamstrings and lower back, and will enable a faster turnover rate. Try "crunches" with legs raised, and "curl ups" with a pelvic tilt. To work the obliques, add a rotation of the torso to each side while doing both of these exercises. Work your way up to three sets of ten reps of each type.

Abdominal Crunches

"Neutral Position" Pelvic tilt with feet together, knees bent and the back flat against the floor.

Lower-Abdominal "Curl -Up"

Side Curl-Up to work the Abdominal Obliques

Around the World

Weights are an integral part of many national teams' training programs. Racewalkers training within the Eastern European, Australian, and U.S. elite programs rely a great deal on weight training, while Mexican and Chinese walkers do very little or no weight work.

It's an individual decision: If you have limited time to train, you'll benefit more from spending the time walking rather than lifting weights. But if you have a few extra hours per week or if you feel that specific

127

muscle weaknesses or strength imbalances are slowing your progress, you should definitely think about getting to the weight room a few days per week.

How to Lift Like a Wimp

My own workouts consist of squats, abdominal and lower back work, plus a lot of presses and other leg weight machines. Although they're great for the beach, pectoralis (chest) and biceps exercises probably aren't going to do much for your racewalking. If I have to wait a few minutes for somebody to get off one of the leg machines, sometimes I'll do a few upper body exercises, but usually I'll spend the time more productively by doing some extra abdominal work.

It's of limited use to name a lot of specific machines here since every weight room is different. Ask the manager of your gym to put together a program for you after showing him or her what racewalking is on the treadmill. If that doesn't get you anywhere, pick up a copy of *Designing Resistance Training Programs* by Fleck and Kramer.

Plyometric Drills

Plyometrics, also known as "bounding drills" or "jump training," are explosive power drills used by many sprinters to develop local muscular strength and explosive power. They are designed to blend speed and strength training, and to build power. Despite being categorized as an endurance event by many coaches, racewalking requires the same type of explosive power that sprinters possess. Without the explosive power of a sprinter, racewalkers would be unable to achieve turnover rates of over 200 strides per minute. Try the following to develop leg strength and power:

> **1. Bounding.** Bounding is an exaggerated running motion, where you "run" with as long a stride as possible; almost like hopping from one foot to the other with very long strides.

> **2. Skipping.** Skip like you did when you were a kid. First skip for height, then for distance.

> **3. Vertical jumps.** Just like it sounds. Jump repeatedly onto and off of a low step or a stable box.

4. Butt kicks. Exaggerate a running in place motion, kicking your butt with your heels.

5. Stadium hops. Simply hop with both feet together up a long flight of stairs as in a track stadium.

Weight training just to look good may build self confidence which can't hurt your walking, but it'll be much more valuable in the long run to use racewalking-specific weight exercises and plyometric drills to develop explosive strength, muscular endurance and injury resistance. Give the weight room a try if you feel you're lacking in any of these areas.

Chapter 24: Cross-Training

Like weight training, cross-training as a supplemental activity can help your walking, but it does not supersede your racewalk training. If you have done your walking work, cross-training can be used to build general endurance while giving the walking muscles a break. It can also be a great tool for continuing to train through a walking injury.

Variety

Your goals should be to build endurance and to reinforce a quick turnover rate while giving your walking muscles a break; your goal should not be to see how good a biker, runner or pogo-stick jumper you can become. Choose cross-training activities that you enjoy: If you like to run, run. If you like to roller blade, roller blade. If you like to bike, bike. But don't overdo any one activity. Use a variety of activities to keep things interesting, and to work more and different muscle groups.

Specificity

Whichever activity you choose, try to make your training as racewalking-specific as possible. U.S. National Racewalk Team members Andrzej Chylinski and Jonathan Matthews both spend a great deal of time each week doing supplemental cross-training activities. And both walkers modify these activities to mimic racewalking's reliance on a high stride frequency. When roller blading, Jonathan uses very short, choppy strokes instead of the long sweeping push-offs that most "serious" roller bladers employ. Andrzej takes very short, quick steps when hiking for hours in the Colorado Rockies. And both walkers put their bikes into a low gear and "spin" with a very high turnover rate when cycling.

Take short, quick steps on the Stairmaster; take short, shuffling steps with a low knee-lift when running; dance to "Limp Bizkit" rather than Vivaldi. Whichever activities you choose, try to modify them to reinforce a very high cadence.

Recovery

Take it easy. The main advantage of cross-training is that it gives your tired walking muscles a break. You're supposed to be recovering from your walking workouts, so don't go nuts. Even though you might be strong enough to walk for two hours, that doesn't mean you'll be able to go out for a two-hour bike ride without causing a lot of soreness in your under-used biking muscles. Start out with a 15-minute ride then see how beat up you are the next day. If you don't feel any undue muscle soreness, build up gradually from there.

Final Thoughts

Some of the best walkers in the world spend hours per week lifting weights, stretching, doing drills, or cross-training. Other elite walkers spend very little time on these activities, but all good walkers walk a lot. With limited hours in the day to train, your walking workouts are the most important workouts you can do to help your walking. But the time you spend racewalking is only one part of a complete workout. You shouldn't even count the mileage if you didn't do your warm up first, then your drills and accelerations, and then your stretches after the walk. Unfortunately, when time is limited, this "supplementary" stuff is the first thing to go. Wrong approach! If your time is limited, you're much better off in the long run if you do 5-10 minutes of drills, 20 minutes of walking, then 5-10 minutes of stretching, rather than walking a longer workout without the drills and stretching.

Don't cut corners—always do "complete" workouts. Then, if you can find the time, do that abominable abdominal work, lift weights, swim and/or cross-train. Doing so will ensure a long, injury-free racewalking career. Ignoring this ancillary work is a sure-fire way to bad technique, sub-par walking times and crippling injuries.

Joanne Dow on:

The Importance of Cross-Training

Accomplishments: 2004 Olympian. 1999, 2002, 2003, 2004 U.S. Indoor 3km champion. 2002 U.S. Outdoor 20km champion. 2003 Pan Am Games bronze medallist. 1997, 1999, 2002 World Cup Team member.

Personal Records:
3 kilometers: 12:36
5 kilometers: 22:40
10 kilometers: 45:36
20 kilometers: 1:32:54

Background: Joanne is a former NCAA Division II national-level collegiate swimmer, who currently works as a personal trainer and as an aerobics and fitness instructor. She teaches walking, rowing, spinning, and muscle-sculpting classes, as well as a variety of aqua, step and traditional aerobics classes. Joanne began racewalking in the spring of 1993. Her base fitness allowed her to progress quickly, but injuries have prevented her from walking as many miles per week as some of her fellow National Team members. Joanne has solved the problem by supplementing her racewalk training with lots of cross-training.

Joanne Says: "Cross-training has been a necessity for me because I tend to suffer frequent racewalking injuries. Because I progressed quickly after starting to racewalk, my body could not keep up with my drive to keep loading the mileage on. I've had to cross-train to give my body a chance to recover between walking workouts. My favorite activity now is the NordicTrak. I also swim a lot during periods of injury, and I like biking—stationary or the real thing. Training in New England always presents climatic challenges for about five months out of the year, so having a cross-training menu to choose from helps me avoid the "no walking blues.""

SECTION V: COMPETITION

THE REWARD FOR YOUR HARD TRAINING

Finally, what it's all about: competition. The moment of truth. The final exam to test the results of all your hard training. Now that you've done the training—you have done the training, haven't you?—the following chapters will deal with acclimatization, final pre-race preparations, various race strategies and other stuff that will help you to get to the finish line before that really obnoxious guy that creeped like heck and beat you at that 5km you did last month.

Chapter 25: Acclimatization

One of the most important, yet least utilized race-preparation tools available to a racewalker is *acclimatization*. Acclimatizing means subjecting the body to environmental conditions similar to those that will be experienced during important races. Acclimatization "tunes" your body to these conditions so you'll be able to work more efficiently during the competition.

The first step to effective acclimatization is reconnaissance. Find out as much as you possibly can about the race: likely weather conditions, time of day and any other variables that may affect your race. Will the competition be at sea level or altitude? Indoors or out? Are the conditions likely to be hot and humid? Is the course hilly or flat? Road or track? Will the race begin at 6:00 a.m. or 5:00 p.m.?

Athletes are often told to ignore these factors because they affect every athlete equally. Once the gun goes off you should tune out these externalities, but since your body is able to adapt to altitude, heat, humidity and other deleterious environmental conditions, you can gain an advantage over your non-acclimated competitors by planning ahead and adapting to these conditions beforehand.

Weather

Extreme heat and humidity inhibit the body's ability to cool itself, forcing the heart to pump lots of blood to the skin instead of to your racewalking muscles. To some degree, the body can acclimate to these conditions. Many of these adaptations occur fairly rapidly, with nearly complete adaptation occurring within 10 to 14 days. By training in hot and humid conditions, or by artificially creating these conditions by wearing sweats during workouts, an athlete can gain an advantage over athletes not specifically preparing for these weather extremes.

British 50km walker, Don Thompson, achieved legendary status due to the wily acclimatization program that prepared him for the hot and humid 1960 Rome Olympics. Training in cool Middlesex, England, Thompson was unable to acclimate on the roads, so several times each week leading up to the Games, Thompson hauled heaters and kettles of boiling water into his bathroom where he did calisthenics in the steaming 100 degree F. heat. After collapsing before the finish of the 1956

Olympic 50km, the heat-adapted Thompson went on to win the Rome 50km. In a similar vein, I've thought about pulling one of the treadmills at my gym into the sauna, but I still haven't figured out a way to get the dang thing up the two flights of stairs. But if I ever do, I'll be ready for anything!

Altitude

Racing at altitudes over 5,000 feet poses a unique challenge for endurance athletes who train at sea level. Unfortunately the only practical way to prepare for a race at altitude is to train in these conditions for at least six weeks before the event. The good news is that most championship races are not held at altitude. But if they do want to race at altitude, sea-level athletes unable to acclimate should plan to race at a pace 7-10% slower than they would be able to maintain at lower elevations.

Since altitude adaptation takes several weeks to set in, there is little point getting into town a week early to try to acclimate. There is even some evidence that getting in as close to the race as possible—perhaps the night before—may be better than getting in several days before.

Going the other way, athletes training at altitude will have difficulty maintaining quick leg turnover during high-elevation workouts, and may be unprepared for the faster pace of sea-level races. These athletes should incorporate sufficient short, fast economy work into their training to adapt to high-speed walking.

Circadian Rhythms

Nothing is more frustrating than going to bed a few hours early for a 6:00 a.m. race, only to lie awake all night tossing and turning with anticipation. Short of tranquilizers, the easiest solution is to retire earlier and earlier in the nights leading up to the race to synchronize the body's internal clock.

Circadian rhythms should also be synchronized by doing workouts in the weeks before the race at or near the time of day that the race will be contested. Many athletes who normally train in the mornings find it difficult to get "up" for an evening race. Afternoon trainers are often tight and tired for morning races. Train at race time to get in synch.

If competing in a different time zone, be sure to calculate the time difference and take this into account when deciding when to sleep or train. As a last resort, I've had a lot of success using melatonin to regulate my sleep patterns when traveling.

While we're on the subject, if you're too excited to sleep the night before the race, don't worry about it. I've walked some of my best times—including my fastest 20km ever—on no sleep. In fact I wasn't able to adjust to the time difference before competing in my personal record 20km in Bekescsaba, Hungary and I lay awake all night for two consecutive nights before the race with no ill effects.

Equipment

Racewalkers require very little equipment to compete, but each athlete should be very comfortable with his shoes, shorts, singlet, Jogbra, etc., before a race. (Did I just say *his* Jogbra?) Always wear your racing shoes and uniform several times in pre-competition training sessions to make certain that you'll be free of blisters or chafing during the race. Also, make sure that you actually have that equipment with you at the starting line! If you tend to be nervous before traveling to a race you may become forgetful. Make a list: shoes, uniform, Mickey Mouse sunglasses, water bottles, extra pins, toilet paper etc., should all be packed and ready to go the night before the race.

Pin your numbers on your uniform as soon as you get them, and racewalk a bit while wearing them to make certain they are pinned on properly. This could save you from frantically re-pinning them at the start line.

Even if it's a cold day, it'll usually feel about 15 degrees warmer once the race starts: Don't overdress! Wear less than you think you'll need, not more. I always wear shorts and a racing top unless it's below 30 degrees. If it's very cold, I may go with a pair of light gloves, but a T-shirt or sweat shirt can become pretty uncomfortable once it's soaked in sweat.

Whatever the weather, don't wear sweat pants, dark-colored or patterned tights, or long shorts while racing. The judges need to see your knees. If they can't, they may just turn in red cards on you without giving you the benefit of the doubt.

I go into more detail in chapter 37, but it *is* a race, right? Be sure to wear your fastest, lightest, most flexible shoes when competing. And don't forget to double-tie the laces and to tuck the ends in between the tongue and the laces. I've double-tied my shoes before some races but still had them come undone because I didn't tuck in my loose ends.

Food and Drink

"Carbo-loading" before major races longer than 90 minutes in duration is advisable. Early proponents suggested a "depletion" phase about a week before the major competition: After a hard glycogen depleting workout, athletes ingested a high-protein, low-carbohydrate diet for two or three days to make the muscles "hungry" for glycogen. They then switched over to a high-carbohydrate diet to "load" the muscles with glycogen. More recent research has determined that the depletion phase is probably unnecessary; you simply need to ingest a high-carbohydrate diet in the three days before the competition without depleting beforehand.

Carbo loading does *not* mean carbo bloating. Carbohydrate percentage should rise a bit beyond the day-to-day standard of 60% carbohydrates, 25% fat, 15% protein level, but total caloric intake does not have to increase. Also, make sure that you have experimented with this type of diet several times in training before attempting to "load" before an important race. Drastic changes in diet may lead to gastric or bowel distress during competition.

In warm races longer than 5km, you'll need to drink on the go. Practice in training! Make sure that you can grab and drink from a cup without stopping. In very long races a carbohydrate-rich sports drink may be necessary, so determine in training what your gut will tolerate; some athletes can't stomach high-carbo drinks while walking. Try with several different types of drinks on your longer workouts to see what works best for you.

Consider a Trial Run

In addition to sharpening your training for a big competition, you should also be putting some thought into logistics. Decide what time you'll leave, who'll be driving, where you'll park, and so on.

A trial run will help you to finalize your plans. If it's a local race, try completing one of your last workouts on the course to test out your race-day plan, and to learn what kind of terrain you'll encounter during the competition. Pack everything you'll take on race day, and head out early enough to get yourself to the course on time. Once you get to the race site, warm up and stretch as usual, then walk the course noting any turns, hills, rough spots on the pavement and anything else that may affect your race.

These are just a few of the things you should keep in mind. As a rule, don't experiment with *anything* during a race. If someone gives you a magic pill the night before the race, don't take it! If it sounds like a good idea, try it in training one or two times first, then try it during an unimportant race. What works for somebody else might not work for you—and you don't want to find that out in the middle of an important race.

What's With the Shades?

I was having trouble concentrating on my warm up before the National 10km at Niagara Falls in 1985 because of a bright glare. I ran into the Ramada Inn gift shop to buy a pair of sunglasses and was faced with the choice of paying $20 for an ugly pair of shades I'd never wear again, or $3 for a pair of pink, 8-year-old kid, Dumbo the Elephant sunglasses. Dumbo it was. They were lightweight, comfortable and cheap, and they worked quite satisfactorily during the race. I have also lost every pair of expensive sunglasses I've ever owned, so I can't justify spending the $80 on "Oakleys" or whatever the heck is popular with the tri-athletes these days.

Anyway, later that year, while living in Southern California, I picked up a couple pair of blue Mickey Mouse glasses at Disneyland. I starting wearing the blue Mickeys in races instead of the not-so-cool pink Dumbos. I've learned that wearing a pair of little-kid shades is a great way to stay relaxed during a stressful race, but they're also lightweight and comfortable, and they stay on really well since they were designed to fit a somewhat smaller face than my own. And at about $3 a pair it's no sweat if I loose a pair or give them away to enthusiastic young spectators when I race overseas.

I'm not a huge Mickey Mouse fan, but since I began wearing the glasses to every race, people assume that I am. My mother, aunts, friends and other athletes have given me dozens of Mickey Mouse T-shirts, hats, socks, pens, watches, etc., over the years. Now I have this enormous collection of Mickey Mouse stuff I'll never use simply because I don't have the heart to tell Mom that I'm just not a die hard Mouseketeer and never really was. (Don't show her this page, okay?)

Chapter 26: Getting There

Let's face it: Despite the occasional rumors of an impending "Walking Boom," there still aren't millions of us racewalkers out there clogging the roads and bike paths of the world. Since we wigglers are still relatively few and far between, you may find it necessary to travel out of town to find good competition. Racing in a national or regional championship can be a great experience. But although you've probably heard from people that haven't "been there" that "getting there" is half the fun, traveling a considerable distance by car or plane to get to a race can take its toll on your body and your mind. This chapter may help to ease some of the hardships of pre-race travel.

Driving

As a National Park Junkie, I love to head out on the highway from time to time for long cross-country road trips. But sitting cramped in a car for an extended period of time can leave you feeling pretty beat up. Maybe I'm being paranoid, but have you noticed how many walkers and walking clubs there are in the Detroit area? I'm beginning to believe that the large number of racewalkers who've infiltrated GM, Ford and Chrysler have specifically designed automobile seats to cripple the rest of us as we drive to compete against them.

If you have to drive for more than an hour or so to get to a race, you *will* wind up trashing your hip flexors, hamstrings and lower back if you're not careful. If the race is more than two hours distant you should think about driving in the day before and staying in a hotel. After checking in, walk for at least 20 minutes, then do your drills, stretch, then finish off with a few accelerations to make sure everything's loosened up.

If you do have to drive more than two hours to get to the race site, be sure to stop every hour or two to stretch and walk around a bit. And if the race is more than an eight-hour drive, you should either break the trip up over two days, or seriously consider flying—there's no way you'll be able to race well if you've beaten yourself up with a marathon drive the day before.

Flying

Getting to a distant race by air presents many of the same challenges as driving, as well as a few that are unique to air travel. Among these are:

1. Dehydration. Most jet cabins are pressurized to the equivalent of about 6,000 to 7,000 feet of altitude, leading to an extremely dry environment. You need to carry a water bottle with you—those little plastic cups of Coke or orange juice aren't going to be enough. Getting up to refill or to use the toilet will also give you a chance to stretch your legs. Selecting an aisle seat will give you the freedom to get up when you need to.

2. Carrying luggage. Chances are, if it's an important race, the airline *will* lose your luggage. You should definitely carry your racing gear on board with you to make sure that you have everything you need to compete, but that doesn't mean you should take *everything* with you onto the plane. If you have a lot of luggage, check the bigger bags so you won't be forced to fatigue your shoulders lugging them through the airport when making connecting flights.

3. Relax! When the airline *does* lose your luggage, the flight is delayed by the weather, or you get seated next to a screaming baby, try to stay calm. Remember chapter 19: If you have no control over the problem, don't let it bother you. If you do, stay calm, and take steps to remedy the unpleasant situation. (Hint: Screaming at the flight attendant is generally *not* the most effective solution to any problems you're likely to encounter.)

4. Time zones. As mentioned earlier, jumping across time zones can be problematic if you let it be. Try to adjust for the time differences in the days before your trip by sleeping and training at appropriate times to synchronize yourself to the new zone.

142

Whatever your mode of transportation to the race, be sure to allow plenty of time for the inevitable delays that crop up on long trips: bad weather, holiday or weekend traffic, airline strikes, natural disasters, cattle on the highway, or extra long lines at the rest stop TCBY counter. By allowing plenty of time for these delays, and getting in a good long warm up before the race, you'll be able to counter many of the ill effects inherent in automobile or air travel.

Victoria Herazo on:
Traveling to Distant Competitions

Accomplishments: 1992 and 1996 Olympian. 1991 and 1997 IAAF World Track & Field Championships Team member. 3-time Pan Am cup and 3-time World Cup Team member. American 15km and 20km record holder. Winner of more than 20 U.S. National Championships—more than any other active American racewalker.

Personal Records:
1 mile:	6:29
3,000 meters:	12:54
5,000 meters:	22:20
10,000 meters:	45:02
20,000 meters:	1:35:39

Background: Tori started racewalking in 1987 after watching Jim Bentley, coaching some young racewalkers in a park near her home in Southern California. Inspired by the young walkers and encouraged by Coach Bentley, Tori gave it a try and took to racewalking immediately. Within two months she qualified to compete in the L.A. Times Indoor Meet where she placed 5th. The next year Tori placed 6th in the women's exhibition racewalk at the '88 Olympic Trials. Then the following year Tori earned the first of more than a dozen berths on U.S. National Team Trips, with a spot on the team representing the U.S. at the Swedish International Walk Week. Through her extensive international experience, and her frequent trips to compete in U.S. National Championships, Victoria has learned a great deal about easing the burdens of long trips to race sites.

Tori Says: "When traveling to a distant race, I try to keep things as simple and as "normal" as possible. I try to get plenty of sleep, eat what I normally eat, and drink a lot of fluids, especially water. I also like to bring a portable tape player so I can relax by listening to my own music instead of what's on the local stations—especially if I'm overseas. That way I can feel "at home" no matter where the race is.

"If I'm driving to a race I try to get out and stretch every hour or two to keep loose, but if the race is more than 300 miles away I'll always fly there. If it's a long flight, I'll get up and stretch on the plane every couple of hours. When I get into town I'll try to stroll around for about 30 minutes of easy racewalking on the race course, then I'll do some "wind sprints" to get the life back into my legs after the trip."

Chapter 27: The Pre-Competition Routine

The first rule of pre-race preparation is to find what works for you and to stick with it. Before an important competition you need to free your mind to concentrate on your race plan; you shouldn't be wasting valuable "mental energy" thinking about pre-competition logistics. Devise a routine that works for you, then use the same method before every competition.

Your race-day preparations should begin well before race morning. If at all possible, pick up your number and registration packet the day before the race. Pin your numbers to your shirt and make sure that the clothes you'll wear during the race fit properly. Get to bed at a reasonable hour the night before—but don't hit the hay much earlier than usual because pre-event jitters may prevent you from falling asleep right away if you try to pack it in too early. I find that reading a good book at bedtime helps me to fall asleep—although a *bad* book may work even better!

On race morning, get up early enough so that you're not rushing around while preparing to go to the course, then be sure to arrive at least 60 minutes before the race to allow yourself plenty of time for registration and for a complete mental and physical warm up.

Use the same pre-competition warm-up routine that you would use before any fast effort: speed and tempo workouts, time trials and ultimately, races. If you do the same warm-up before all your hard workouts, it will be automatic come race day.

The following routine will get you to the starting line loose, warmed up, and ready to go:

> **1. Warm up.** An easy 10 to 20 minute racewalk, or a combination of jogging then walking will help to work out the kinks and pump some blood into the muscles to facilitate drills and stretching.

> **2. Dynamic flexibility drills.** Perform five or ten minutes of drills from chapter 22 to prepare your neuromuscular system and extend the range of motion of your walking muscles.

3. Accelerations. Three or four 40- to 50-meter accelerations will further enhance the range of motion of your racewalking-specific muscles. Be sure to get up to race speed to make sure your technique feels good at competition pace.

4. Stretch any "problem" areas. If anything still feels uncomfortable, spend a few minutes stretching the tight spots.

5. Go! But don't go nuts. You're warmed up, loose, and full of adrenaline—start the race at what feels like a very comfortable pace and you'll probably be right on. Go out too hard and you'll pay for it in the second half of the race.

When you find a pre-race routine that works for you and use it every time you race, you'll always be loose, relaxed and ready to go. The last thing you want to do is show up at the starting line stressed-out because you're still tying your shoes and pinning your number on when the gun goes off. Not that that's ever happened to me....

Chapter 28: Racing Strategies

There are a number of different ways to pace yourself through a race. You can go out hard and hang on as long as you can, you can try to maintain a steady pace, or you can try to start out at a comfortable pace then go faster and faster throughout the race to "negative split."

Blast & Burnout

This is the strategy of choice for the rank beginner; the guy in the black socks and Bermuda shorts who leads the New York Marathon for the first 100 meters, then winds up flooded with lactate, curled up in a fetal position next to a fire hydrant somewhere in Queens. The idea is to go out hard to break your competitors, then to hang on as long as you can—hopefully to the finish line. That only works if you're far superior to your competitors anyway, in which case you would have won no matter what strategy you used. If you like lactic acid and *rigor mortis*, this is the strategy for you; if you like personal records and winning races, don't even think about it.

Steady Pace

Remember the Tortoise and the Hare? (Hint: The Turtle wins.) If you've done your track intervals and tempo walks you should have a pretty good idea of the pace you'll be able to handle for the race distance. The goal here is to start out at that pace and carry it through to the finish line. By walking a steady pace you should be pretty comfortable through most of the race, only feeling physiological stress in the final stages—if you've judged your starting pace correctly.

Negative Split

Most championship races are won by a negative-splitting walker, one who takes the pace out relatively conservatively then accelerates throughout the race. This strategy gives the body a good chance to warm up in the early going, and allows you to save the hardest walking for the end. To negative split you should start out just a little bit conservatively, letting the other walkers fight for position in the first few kilometers. Then you consciously accelerate throughout the race by slightly increasing your turnover rate every lap. Since things will be getting tougher and tougher over the last few kilometers, and your stride rate may be decreasing from muscle tightness, you may not actually be picking the pace up very much, but the end of the race will still *feel* much faster. This strategy is very good psychologically since you'll be passing other walkers throughout the race.

Stick & Kick

Sticking and kicking—hanging on to another walker's pace throughout the race then blowing by them at the end—is a very "easy" strategy since the other walker does all the pacing work. It's a good way of taking some of the stress out of racing, but it does have its flaws. First, you're saving yourself for a big kick at the end, which could lead to disqualification. Then because you've saved all your effort for that kick your finishing time may not be as fast as it would have been if you had pushed the pace the whole way—and you can never be completely certain that you'll actually be able to out-kick your rival. Despite the drawbacks, if your goal is simply to beat a particular rival, and you're confident that you have a fast, *legal* finishing kick, this strategy may be a viable option for you.

Whichever race strategy you choose, look at the race tactically. Break it down into sections, then concentrate on a different sub-strategy in each. Chapter 29 will show you how to break the race down into different phases where you'll first focus on control, then on maintaining pace, and finally on hammering home to the finish line.

Chapter 29: Control, Maintain, and Hammer

Any race, of any distance, can be broken down into three sections, each with a different focus. The first third of the race your thoughts should be on staying in *control,* the second on working to *maintain* the pace, the final third on fighting the fatigue and negative thoughts and making sure you *hammer* all the way to the finish.

First Third of the Race: "Control"

You can't win a race in the first third, but you may very well lose it if you go out too hard. The first third of the race is a time to control your emotions—and your speed. Adrenaline will "tell you" to go out like a maniac. Ignore that voice or you'll be wallowing in lactate before long. Everybody on that starting line is feeling the same way you are. And most people respond by starting out *way* too fast. Let them go: They will come back before long.

Middle Third of the Race: "Maintain"

It is imperative to stay focused during the second third of the race. It's very easy to "fall asleep" during the middle part of the race: This is when you need to stay alert to keep yourself from letting the pace drop off, and letting competitors pull away from you. When someone you've been walking with puts on a surge, it's very easy to say, "I'll catch up to him later." The "rational" side of your brain doesn't want you to walk fast; it wants to sit in the shade and have a cold beer while all those other nuts battle it out. You need to keep that side of your brain down with "self-talk," letting the "I want a personal record, I want a medal, I want to win this thing" side of your brain rise to the top.

It's important to keep your turnover rate up. I do so by listening to a "metronome" in my head: After spending hours on the track preparing for your races by doing race-pace intervals, your neuromuscular system should have that pace locked in, giving you a pretty good sense of what it feels like. If it feels or "sounds" like your cadence is falling off, pick it up. If you feel like you're not working very hard, get moving. By now you should be passing those knuckleheads who went out too hard. Use these small victories to stoke your confidence.

Final Third of the Race: "Hammer"

This is it: hammer time! Time to put it into high gear and make it hurt. If you've gone out too hard it'll be impossible for you to accelerate now; if you started at a reasonable pace, this should be the fastest part of the race. Don't make any sudden moves; accelerate smoothly so you don't put yourself in danger of lifting. And don't save it for the final 100 meters—you should be really working the entire final third of the race so that you approach the finish line almost spent.

Chapter 30: Racing Smart—Using Your Head to Get Ahead

Whether you like to go out hard, maintain a steady pace, or accelerate through the race, there will always be opportunities during the race to use the course or the judges to your advantage. This chapter will show you how walking *smarter* can improve your times as much as walking *harder* can.

Walking the Shortest Path

Everybody in the race will start at the same start line and finish at the same finish line. But not everyone will take exactly the same path between those points. Most walkers will follow the road wherever it goes, like lemmings to the sea. If there are cones marking the course, most walkers will follow the gently curving line of the cones—and they'll wind up walking 200 meters farther than the smart walkers who *cut the tangents.*

The shortest distance between two points is a straight line, so stay alert. If the next turn in the race is a left and you're on the right-hand side of the road, you need to cut a straight-line path across the road to get there. If there's a water stop on the other side of the road, don't cut over at the last minute, plan ahead and start cutting over as soon as you see it off in the distance. The shortened distances can really add up over the course of a five- or ten-kilometer race.

Cutting the tangents is not "cheating"—race courses are measured along the tangents. If you *don't* cut the tangents you'll actually be walking *longer* than the certified race distance.

Handling Hills

Hills are another feature of a course that can either help you or hammer you, depending on how you handle them. You need to be aggressive going up hills, but you can't expect to maintain the same pace on a hill that you would on the flat parts of the course. Try to maintain a *constant effort* going up the incline so you don't send your heart rate skyrocketing. Since your stride length will be shortened on the way up the hill, you'll usually be able to maintain a relatively constant effort by simply maintaining your turnover rate—even though your pace will be slowed somewhat by the shortened stride.

Whatever you do, stay relaxed and maintain your form: Keep a good erect posture, bring your arms up just a little bit higher, and make sure you maintain that short, quick, efficient turnover rate all the way to the top and beyond the crest of the hill.

Whatever happens, relax. If your competitors push too hard on the way up the hill, let them go. They'll die by the time they reach the top, and you'll be able to catch them on the way down. If you haven't blown all your energy on the way up, it'll be a snap to walk fast on the down side. Take advantage of the free energy you'll get from gravity's pull; go fast, but concentrate on staying efficient and legal.

The trick to downhill walking is *controlling* your pace. Since the hill will be falling away in front of you, you'll actually have to extend your lead leg out to the front a bit to keep yourself from spinning out of control. You also need to stay legal on the downslope, so hold your arms a bit lower to keep your center of gravity down. Practice racewalking both up and down hills in training: Learning the proper technique before the race will keep you legal and injury-free during the race.

Handling the Judges

The judges were mentioned earlier in regard to your own technique, but they can be important tools to use against your competitors if you're very confident of your own legality. Other walkers may not share your confidence; take this into account. When you see a judge up ahead, push the pace a little. One of two things will happen: Your competitor will let you go, afraid that by keeping up he'll lose his technique in front of the judge; or he'll try to go with you, putting himself in danger of receiving a red card from the judge. Be sure to position yourself on the far side of your competitor—not to "hide" your own excellent technique from the judge, but to give him a better look at your rival's ragged technique!

Using the Turns

Most racewalks are held on out-and-back loop courses to give the judges several chances to see each competitor. But the loop courses also give the competitors a chance to see *each other*. If you're ahead of another walker, you'll be able to see just how far ahead you are right after you make each turn. As soon as you make the turn, time how long it takes for you to get even with the other walker as he approaches the turn and you pull away. Double that time to determine your lead: If you pass each other 10 seconds after you hit the turn around, you're 20 seconds ahead.

The other walker will be gauging your lead as well, so as soon as you pass him—and he can't see you—pick up the pace for a few minutes. Your rival won't know what hit him when he rounds the turn and finds you *gone*, 30 seconds ahead!

If, on the other hand, *you're* trying to catch another walker, he'll get a good look at *you* after he makes the turn. Try to look as unthreatening as possible: Put your head down, look exhausted, then, as soon as you pass each other and his back is to you, pull yourself together again and put on a hard surge. You'll be "invisible" walking behind the other walker, so he won't see how much ground you've gained until the next turn around. And by then it'll be too late: you'll be right there behind him ready to go in for the kill!

Andrew Hermann on:
Smart Racing, Smart Pacing

Accomplishments: 2000 Olympian at 50 kilometers. 1997 National 50km Champion. 1997 and 1999 IAAF World Championships Team member. 2nd at the 1996 and 2000 U.S. Olympic 50km Trials. 1995, '97, and '99 World Cup Team member and 1994 and '96, '98 and 2000 Pan Am Cup Team member.

Personal Records:
5 kilometers: 20:50
10 kilometers: 42:30
20 kilometers: 1:26:07
50 kilometers: 3:58:52

Background: Andrew began racewalking in 1989 as a college freshman. A 32-minute 10km runner for the Willamette University cross-country and track teams, Andrew wanted to earn additional points for his school in the 10km racewalk at the NAIA National Championships.

After a successful four years at Willamette, Andrew moved to the U.S. Olympic Training Center in Lake Placid, New York, his mind set on becoming an Olympian like his cousin, Olympic gold and silver medal-winning discus thrower, Mac Wilkins. Unhappy with his progress, Andrew moved to the racewalking "Center of Excellence" in LaGrange, Georgia in 1994. He thrived in LaGrange, earning spots on several international teams, and nearly winning the 1996 Olympic 50km Trial. Disappointed at barely missing a spot on the Olympic Team, Andrew decided to move once again, this time to Barcelona, Spain, to train at the Spanish Olympic Training Center.

After training hard and learning a great deal about pacing and racing strategies from his Olympic and World Champion training partners, Andrew finally reached the pinnacle of U.S. racewalking by winning the 1997 50km National Championship and competing in the 50km at the 2000 Olympic Games.

Andrew says:
"In my first 50km at the 1995 National Championship, I went out too

fast and crashed badly. I still hadn't learned my lesson by the 1996 Olympic Trials and I think it may have cost me a spot on the Olympic Team. Finally, after training with the Spaniards, I learned that to walk four hours for 50km, you have to start out at 4:05 pace and then accelerate through the race. The first 30-35kms have to be very comfortable or you'll end up crashing over the last 10-15kms.

"The key is to go out conservatively and to work into the race. That way you feel much better in the early stages, then you spend the last half of the race passing all your competitors which is very good psychologically.

"I realize that most walkers don't race 50km, but what's true for the 50km is also true for 20kms, tens, and even fives: Negative-splitting is the surest strategy for success. Look at [1997 20km World Champion] Daniel Garcia. He went out very comfortably and let the lead group set the pace. He didn't waste any energy jostling for position or covering the other walkers' surges. He just sat back and surveyed the situation, staying calm and relaxed over the first 10 kilometers, moving up through the pack from 10 to 15 kilometers, then hammering everyone into the ground over the final 5km.

"Whether you're an elite 50km walker or a beginning 5km walker, there are going to be days where you're "on" and days when you're not. If you start out easy and see how it goes, with the ultimate goal of always picking it up and accelerating throughout the race, you'll do well no matter what kind of day you're having. If you start out the other way around you *may* have a decent race, but you may also wind up crashing and having a *really* bad day.

"Another thing to keep in mind is that you're going to be in pain one way or another, so you need to expect that, but it's much better to hurt in the closing stages of the race than to hurt in the middle part of the race after going out too hard, and then to come crawling into the finish line slow and exhausted.

"Andrzej Chylinski once told me something that I think is true for any race distance. He said you must race the first half of the race with your brain, and the second half with your heart. In other words, go out at a conservative pace at the start, patiently letting the others fight it out in the early going, then have the courage and mental toughness to really push things in the closing stages of the race. That, I think, is the key to successful racing: patience and the ability to accelerate through the race."

156

Chapter 31: To Drink or Not to Drink...

It's generally not worthwhile to drink anything during races shorter than 10 kilometers. It takes about 20 minutes for your body to absorb the drink, so nothing ingested in the final stages of the race has time to reach your bloodstream. Since it's not going to have time to help you, you'll just be wasting your time reaching for that cup and drinking.

I've actually been told by Chinese and Byelorussian coaches that it's not necessary to drink during *any* race of 20 kilometers or shorter. I think their view is an extreme one, but I didn't drink a drop during my fastest 20km race ever. The temperature during that particular race was in the low 30s, though, so dehydration wasn't really a factor. In general, I would recommend drinking in races of 10 kilometers or longer, especially if it's a warm day.

What to Drink

In most cases, cold water is your best bet, since it is absorbed much faster than sports drinks containing sugars. These sugars can also lead to insulin spikes and "crashes" that may harm your performance. But in longer races—those lasting 90 minutes or more—sugar can be very helpful. Glycogen depletion can be a very real problem even in hard 20km races, so sports drinks can be used as a fuel to conserve intra-muscular and blood glycogen.

If you're thinking about using sports drinks, don't drink them within two hours of racing or else insulin could cause a blood-sugar "crash" before or during the race. It is, however, alright to drink the sports drink *immediately* before the start of the race because the sugars will be burned directly without initiating an insulin response.

Early and Often

If you're competing in a longer race, don't wait until you're thirsty to start drinking—by then it'll be too late. As you get dehydrated, blood flow to the stomach and intestines is reduced so that the majority of your available oxygen can be shunted to the working muscles. The stomach doesn't work as efficiently with the reduced blood supply, so most of the water you do ingest after dehydration sets in just sits there, sloshing around with bile and stomach acid. I'm told that's why I tend to vomit so

157

much during hot-weather races and workouts. I dehydrate easily and lose the ability to absorb any of the water I ingest. It ain't a pretty thing, so in longer races drink early and often!

Final Thoughts

After spending countless hours training it would be a waste to be less than 100% ready to race because you haven't acclimated or you've "blown your taper" by pushing too hard in the final weeks before the competition. Success has as much to do with using your brain as with using your brawn. You really need to step back and objectively assess everything you do leading up to a race: Does it make sense to drive 12 hours to get there the night before? Should you eat that strange new "energy bar" the morning of the race because everybody else is? Then, during the race, you need to keep your head by not starting out too fast, walking the shortest distance on the course, using the judges to your advantage, and being alert and responsive to what your competitors are doing.

I'll say it again: Don't be a bonehead! Stick with what has worked in training, and race smart, and you'll have a huge advantage over the 95% of your competitors who end up doing all kinds of crazy things before and during important races.

SECTION VI: LOOSE ENDS

SOME THINGS TO MAKE YOUR TRAINING EASIER AND MORE INTERESTING

The following chapters are a mixed bag of useful information that didn't quite fit into the preceding sections: special concerns for youth and masters athletes; nutrition; injuries; equipment like shoes, treadmills and heart rate monitors; recruiting good potential walkers, that sort of thing. Hey, it was either this or 50 pages of appendices.

Chapter 32: Special Concerns for Younger Racewalkers

The easiest way to turn potential young racewalking stars into burned-out flashes in the pan is to push them too hard. Kids need encouragement, they don't need bullwhips or nagging. That may sound like a page straight out of Dr. Spock, but if it's not fun they're not going to stick with it.

I love coaching kids. It's a real treat when I get to work with young, enthusiastic walkers. But I've had to rehabilitate too many battle-fatigued veterans of youth sports who've been run through the wringer by overzealous parents and coaches.

Our national youth program needs to foster and encourage these young athletes, but we have had a history of trying to force an unrealistic work ethic upon very young walkers that winds up being too much for them. It's great to see fast times from precocious 14-year olds, but not at the expense of losing these athletes forever six months down the road due to injuries or burnout.

Variety

The life of a competitive racewalker can be a lonely existence. It's very likely that you'll spend a lot of time training on your own and that people around you aren't going to understand what it is that you're trying to accomplish. This can be a real problem for kids, many of whom feel the need to "fit in."

Before the age of 16 or so, racewalking should be a strictly part-time activity. Some of the closest friends I've ever had were those from my high school cross-country and track teams. It would be unfair to cut a young athlete off from these life experiences by demanding that they focus solely on racewalking. It's perfectly acceptable for a youth-level racewalker to run cross-country or to play tennis or soccer in the fall and to mix racewalking training with membership on the school track team, or even the chess club or debating team during the spring. Whatever it takes to keep it fun. (The debating team *is* fun, isn't it, or is that debatable?)

Training

A young walker's training should center on building endurance with easy eight- to ten-kilometer walks, and developing technique with drills and supervised economy intervals. Occasional tempo walks and threshold intervals to prepare for competition are also acceptable, but these workouts should not be over-emphasized.

Distance work. Even though racewalking is growing in popularity and acceptance as a "real" athletic pursuit, many young walkers still feel self-conscious about training out on the roads. I may have achieved a certain amount of success in the sport over the years, but I still have insults—along with an occasional beer bottle—hurled at me from time to time during my workouts. Nothing fazes me anymore, but to a young walker this can be pretty disconcerting.

One of the most helpful things a parent or coach can do for these kids is to drive them to a park with a bike path or out to a quiet country road where they can do their long workouts. Anyplace where runners gather can usually be considered a "safe haven" for a racewalker—other athletes understand commitment to a goal a lot more than the average person you'll run into out on an "unprotected" road workout.

Distance work should be a mix of easy and harder 5 to 15 kilometer walks, including at least one steady-state or acceleration tempo walk per week. Younger walkers shouldn't walk any more than about 15km on their long days, and no more than about 50 to 60 total kilometers per week.

Technique training. A few days per week should be designated as "technique days" where supervised technique work, drills, and fast economy intervals of up to 400 meters are performed on the track. These short intervals should be walked with perfect technique—as economy intervals, not as punishing VO_2 max intervals.

Whenever walking intervals longer than 200 meters, the pace should be limited to race pace. Too many young walkers, shy about walking on the roads, resort to walking excessive VO_2-type intervals several times per week, without doing sufficient distance work. Technique, endurance, and speed-endurance must be the focus of a young walker's training.

Sharpening. About six weeks before the start of racing season, one threshold interval workout should be added to the weekly schedule. 600- to 1,200-meter intervals with 2-minute recoveries, adding up to no more than 5km of work, are appropriate. These intervals should be walked at no faster than 5km race pace.

Competition

Most racing opportunities for youth walkers are in the 1,500-meter to 5km range; fortunate because it "forces" kids to learn to walk with a quick turnover rate. Emphasis on the shorter races is also good because training for these races requires less physical, mental and time commitment than the longer races. Learning to walk fast over short distances is an important skill that is best learned as early in a walker's career as possible. The endurance to translate that speed to longer— Olympic—distances will come with time. But if you try to push a young walker to do too much too soon they'll never have the chance to get to that level.

Over-burdened walkers will quit the sport long before they've gained the physical maturity required to be competitive in the open 10km, 20km and 50km races. Keep the competition fun and low key, and if there's a future star in there, the talent will eventually reveal itself.

Josh Ginsburg on:
Special Concerns for Younger Racewalkers

Accomplishments: Junior American record holder for the 5km road walk (22:25). Runner-up at the 1995 National Scholastic 5km Championship. 1995 (track) and 1996 (road) junior national 5km champion. 3rd at the 1996 Junior National 10km Championship, 2nd at the 1996 USA vs. Canada junior dual meet.

Personal Records:
1 mile: 6:32
3,000 meters: 12:27
5,000 meters: 21:21
10,000 meters: 46:22

Background: Josh started racewalking as a freshman at Huntington (NY) High School. He walked 9:20 for the mile his freshman year, then dropped to 7:23 his sophomore year after picking up some technique and training tips from a U.S. National Team racewalker. (Oh, alright, it was me!) By his senior year, Josh had attended two Dave's World Class clinics, improved his technique dramatically, and brought his mile time down to 6:53.

After graduating, Josh attended Mary Washington College in Fredericksburg, VA and commuted to the USA Track & Field Northern Virginia Center of Excellence, where he was able to train with Phillip Dunn, Mary-Kirk Cunningham, and other elite walkers. His times continued to improve, but the one-track focus of the program led to injuries and a case of "burn out," halting his progress. Josh transferred to the University of Mobile in the fall of 1997, to become the first racewalker on the NAIA school's track team.

Josh says: "I made some big jumps early on by working with a good coach, and really concentrating on technique. Then, when I was able to train with other walkers at the Center of Excellence, I continued to improve, but there were a lot of problems for a young walker training in such an intense environment. There was too much emphasis on speed work, so there were a lot of injuries. And worse, there was just way too much pressure—especially for the younger walkers. Walking was *everything*. I really enjoyed running cross-country in high school, but we weren't allowed to run, or to do anything that didn't directly relate to our walking: Fun was *bad*.

"It's important to train hard, but it's equally important to enjoy what you're doing. A lot of younger walkers have early successes, then get pushed too hard to excel by their high school coaches or parents. Younger walkers in particular need a positive coach. I had a lot of problems working under a coach who was very negative; who criticized everything that I did. If I had a good workout, it wasn't good enough. If I had a 30-second PR it should have been a minute. If I got injured, It was 'all in my head.'

"Overall, I think the most important things for young walkers are to:

1.) Enjoy what you're doing.
2.) Find a coach who understands that you want to walk well, *and* you want to have fun doing it.
3.) Seek out advice from good walkers and coaches, but *filter it.* Make sure it makes sense, and when you find something that works, stick with it.
4.) Stay focused: Train consistently.
5.) Go easy on the speed work. It'll make you faster in the short run, but you'll wind up burned out or injured before long.
6.) Work on your technique *every* day.

"It's great to make big improvements as a teenager, but very few teenage racewalkers make Olympic Teams. You'll get faster as you get older and stronger, but only if you stick with it. If you do *too* much early on, you'll burn out and quit before you ever have a chance to walk any *really* fast times."

Chapter 33: Special Concerns for Older Racewalkers

Masters athletes need to be more concerned with overtraining and injuries than their younger counterparts. Age itself has a lot to do with these problems, but the "grown-up" lifestyle is equally to blame. Job and family commitments leave precious little time for training, let alone for adequate rest, stretching and other "preventative maintenance."

If You Think You're Old, You Are

Another problem with some older athletes is that they *think* they're old. It may take a little bit longer to recover from your workouts, and you may need to spend more time stretching, doing drills, and getting massage and other body work, but there's no reason to think of yourself as any less of an *athlete* than walkers half your age. Over the years, there have been plenty of athletes over forty good enough to make the Men's and Women's U.S. National Racewalk Teams. In fact, three members of the five-man 50km team representing the U.S. at the '97 World Cup in Podebrady, Czech Republic were over forty—34-year-old Andrzej Chylinski was the "baby" of the squad.

These racewalkers don't excel because they think of themselves as masters athletes, they excel because they see themselves as athletes, period. Jim Carmines, an American record holder in the 50+ age group, says he keeps himself motivated by trying to beat everyone over the age of 40—and most of the under-40 crowd as well. Steve Feith, a masters walker living in Tampa, FL, will often "drop down" into a *younger* age group to find better competition. Don't put limitations on yourself because you're chronologically a 50-, 60-, or 70-year-old walker. Define yourself as an *athlete*—not as a number on your social security card.

The Song Remains the Same

The rules don't change once you hit 40. You still need to train hard, and to counter that hard training with easy recovery workouts. You still need to train consistently, and to do that long day. And you can't rush things—you may think that your days as an athlete are numbered, but if anything you need to give yourself *more* time to reach your goals than a younger walker would. Luckily, with age you tend to shed some of the impetuousness of youth and gain the wisdom to take those easy days when you need them, and to back off when you feel a cold or an injury coming on. Take advantage of that wisdom: Think long-term, work hard and rest easy and you'll reach any goals you set for yourself.

Jonathan Matthews on:
Special Concerns for Older Racewalkers

Accomplishments: 1993 National 50km Champion, 1994 National Indoor and Outdoor 5km Champion. Former American record holder for the 3km and one-hour outdoor track racewalks. Masters (over 40 years old) record holder at all distances from 5km to 50km.

Personal Records:
3 kilometers: 11:26
5 kilometers: 20:01
10 kilometers: 41:45
20 kilometers: 1:24:43
50 kilometers: 4:01:36

Background: Jonathan was a talented track runner who ran 1:57 for the 1/2 mile in high school while often injured. As a freshman in college he ran 1:55 for 800 meters but soon switched to bicycling due to chronic Achilles tendonitis. He rose quickly to the top of the cycling world, earning a spot on the National Cycling Team, but retired after several life-threatening crashes. Unable to remain idle, Jonathan started racewalking in 1990 at the age of 34, again rising to the top of the heap: He was 6th at the 1991 World Cup 20km Trials, and 3rd at 1992 U.S. Olympic 20km Trials. Since turning 40 in 1996 Jonathan has made a hobby of taking down every masters record in existence from 5km to 50km.

Jonathan Says: "Since I became a masters walker while still racing at the upper levels of U.S. open competition, I've been able to achieve a bit more success than is normally possible at this age. This simply confirms that with a sufficiently athletic background and a disciplined approach to training, masters athletes can walk very fast. Don DeNoon of the U.S. and Gary Little of New Zealand have shown what is possible. At age 50, DeNoon was walking 5km and 20km at the same speed he achieved while competing as a 20-year old. In his late 40s Gary Little was walking 20km in 1:27. In absolute terms, advancing age limits performance. However, if you train well, you are going to race very fast.

"A masters walker usually cannot handle more than three hard workouts a week, alternating at least one easy day for every hard day. In fact, it is possible to race successfully on only three days of racewalking per week. Non-impact cross training (cycling, skating, stepping, regular walking) can be used on the other four days of the week. On this schedule, your walking efforts must be very focused: typically two speed efforts and one long effort.

"When properly prepared, masters walkers can continue to handle intense training efforts, but they must cut back on less-intense "bulk mileage." You must continue to work very hard on hard days, but get much more recovery/rest between these hard efforts than would be typical for a younger athlete. Also very important as you get older: Maintain/increase strength with hill repetitions and maintain/increase flexibility with at least 20 minutes of stretching a day."

Chapter 34: Nutrition

The fats and carbohydrates in the food we eat are used by the body as fuels when training and racing, while protein goes into rebuilding muscles and blood cells. Obviously then, athletes need to be concerned with what goes into their bodies.

Having said that, I've been a PopTart and Cap'n Crunch-aholic throughout my entire competitive career, and I won't even think twice about eating a greasy cheeseburger two hours before any race shorter than 20km. I believe that when training mileage and intensity are high, caloric intake is generally high enough to supply the body with sufficient protein, carbohydrates, fats, vitamins and minerals. You definitely need to keep yourself hydrated by drinking constantly, but otherwise I'm the wrong person to be asking about nutrition.

I do actually have lots of books and clippings on proper dietary guidelines for athletes, but for me to write about such things would be the height of hypocrisy. There are, however, a few things I'd feel guilty about months from now if I didn't mention them; things I've learned to do and not do over the years. Among these:

Vitamins

Be *very* careful with these things. Back in 1991 and '92 I was sponsored by an independent vitamin manufacturer. I began feeling really fatigued while training for the 1991 World Cup Trials so my vitamin guy suggested I take 200mg of this and 400mg of that. I got worse, so he told me to take more supplements. I only got better when I forgot to take my pills to California for the trials race. A similar thing happened the following year in the weeks before the 1992 Olympic Trials, so I had some blood work done and discovered that my liver had all but shut down, clogged as it was with fat-soluble vitamins, iron, zinc, magnesium and other metals.

Very few people are walking around these days with rickets or scurvy. Vitamin and mineral deficiencies are the exception not the rule, so avoid taking supplements unless you're sure there is a problem—and certain that vitamin or mineral supplements will cure rather than exacerbate the problem.

A daily multivitamin is probably safe for most people, and women may want to think about taking a daily with iron, but beyond that, get blood work done before trying to cure your real or imagined ailments with pills.

Ergogenics

No, not the L. Ron Hubbard book; *ergogenics* are (legal or illegal) nutritional supplements taken in the hopes of enhancing athletic performance. Legal ergogenics include bee pollen, coenzyme Q_{10}, blue-green algae, shark cartilage and that sort of thing. If you really believe that spending $30 on a bottle of eye of newt will help your race, there probably will be some placebo effect, but there's no evidence that any of this stuff works.

Water

Well-hydrated muscles are strong and flexible; dehydrated muscles are as flexible as beef jerky or shoe leather. Drink constantly to avoid getting these dried out, injury-prone muscles. Keep a water bottle with you all the time during the day, drink 6-8 ounces every 15 minutes while training, and be sure to begin rehydrating immediately after training— even while you're stretching. Water is cheap, safe, and readily available. The only downside is that you may have to take a number of quick bathroom breaks during the day, but you can do so while your co-workers are out slacking off taking their cigarette breaks.

Carbos

Be sure to "carbo load" for long races and workouts by eating a slightly higher-than-normal percentage of carbohydrates—about 70-75%—in the two to four days before the long effort. Doing so will ensure that your muscles are fully loaded with glycogen for the race or workout.

These long workouts and races deplete the body of carbohydrates. The most effective way to "reload" is to ingest some kind of sports drink within 15 minutes of completing the workout, and then to have a more substantial high-carbo meal within the next two hours. Adding a small amount of protein to your meal—perhaps 15% of total calories—will aid in carbohydrate absorption.

Variety

Try to eat a variety of wholesome foods from the Five Basic Food Groups daily. These are (according to Mark Fenton):

1. Beer and beer supplements. Supplements include anything salty, like pretzels, potato chips, popcorn, cheese doodles, etc.

2. Deliverables, such as pizza, and Chinese food, as well as anything that can be ordered from the face of a clown, like burgers, fries and shakes.

3. Meat-like substances. These include such digestion-resistant favorites as beef jerky, hot dogs, pepperoni, salami, and of course, Spam.

4. PopTarts and other toaster pastries.

5. Simple sugars. Also known as "sinful sugars." Why make things complicated? Stick to *simple* carbs like ice cream and Cap'n Crunch instead of getting bogged down by those nasty, complicated *complex* carbohydrates.

Or perhaps you'd like to refer to the USDA version.... For more information on nutrition for athletes, pick up a copy of *Nancy Clark's Sports Nutrition Guidebook* or *The Athlete's Kitchen*, or visit the American Dietetic Association's website at www.eatright.org.

Chapter 35: Treadmills

Although I certainly wouldn't recommend using them every day, treadmills can be a valuable training tool when the conditions outside become unbearable. I certainly prefer training outdoors, but for dangerous weather days—freezing rain or life-threatening heat and humidity—you can't beat 'em. Treadmills can also be used for physiological testing, for trying out new technique changes, or as a change of pace if you live in a very flat, or an excessively hilly location. If you have your own treadmill, or access to a health club's treadmills, try some of the following:

Escaping the Weather

I rarely skip a day because of the weather—although there are some days I wish had. I broke my leg slipping on ice during a workout in 1984, and I've had more hot-weather workouts than I'd care to think about cut short by unpleasant vomiting episodes, so I'm not above escaping from the weather by heading indoors when the weather conditions get really tough.

Tempo workouts are the best candidates for indoor workouts. It can sometimes be tough to maintain focus throughout a tough steady-state or acceleration tempo, but with the belt controlling the pace you don't have to. And on hot, humid days you'll never be able to maintain a fast pace without your heart rate going through the roof; the cooler, dryer indoor environment will allow you to walk at a much faster pace while staying in your 80-85% tempo workout heart rate range.

Adding or Avoiding Hills

Hill repeats can be a great tool for working on efficient technique, building racewalking-specific strength, or just getting your heart rate up. But a lot of walkers I coach in places like South Florida and New Orleans don't have any hills on which to train. Lots of other walkers, myself included, can't seem to get away from the hills.

The problem with *too many* hills is that you can't really get into a rhythm during your workouts. It helps to be able to maintain good race-specific technique during your workouts—your technique can begin to suffer if you can't walk on the flats for extended bouts several times per week. And since few races are contested on hills because they can make it tough to avoid lifting on the downhill sections, hills don't really help your race-specific technique if you can't get away from them to train on the flats from time to time. Non-stop hill work can also cause injuries because it's very tough on the hamstrings and lower back.

If walking in your neighborhood is more like a roller coaster ride than a workout, try heading indoors a few days per week for your tempo workouts and perhaps for a few easy walks. If, on the other hand, you can't find any hills near you try jacking up the incline on the machine to 4 or 5% for a dose of technique, strength, or VO_2 work.

"Tweaking" Technique

There are a number of ways a treadmill can help you to refine your technique.

> **1. Instant feedback.** By keeping you in one place, a treadmill can allow you to see yourself in real-time while you walk. Setting up mirrors or hooking up a video camera to a television can afford you instant visual feedback.

> **2. Steady hills.** Controlled hill repeats force you to push off with a more pronounced ankle flexion behind you. They also make you cut your stride in front of your body. Both are elements of good racewalk technique. It's always better to do hill repeats outdoors, but if you don't have any hills, treadmills offer a good substitute.

> **3. Efficiency test.** A treadmill can give you precise control over your speed enabling you to determine the most efficient between a number of different racewalking styles. When testing a minor technique change I'll head to the gym with a heart rate monitor so I can gauge which variations are the most efficient. The treadmill controls the speed, and the room temperature and humidity are pretty stable from one minute to the next, so technique efficiency is really the only variable that will effect heart rate. Simply walk at a steady pace until heart rate stabilizes, then make the technique changes. A more efficient technique will lead to a drop in heart rate; a less efficient one will lead to a rise.

Testing Your Ticker

There are a number of fancy-schmancy, ultra high-tech, hoses sticking out of your nose, blood being sucked out of your veins treadmill tests that exercise physiologists can perform on you to determine how well each of your systems are running. There are also tests that you can do for yourself using a treadmill and a heart rate monitor, including the Conconi test which is a very easily performed test used to determine heart rate and walking speed at lactate threshold.

I'd love to tell you all about the Conconi and other tests, but description of the protocols goes beyond the scope of this work. (I've always wanted to write that "beyond the scope of this work" thing on something without getting points taken off. Thanks for reading along.) If you own a higher-end model heart rate monitor, one the can download data to a computer, the user's manual should describe the Conconi and other tests.

Chapter 36: Heart Rate Monitors

I've read a number of "What the Heck's the Use" articles on heart rate monitors, written by coaches who believe that athletes should just run slow on their easy days, and fast on their hard days, and that they don't need a $200 gizmo to tell them that. But most of the athletes that I work with have never had the benefit of a good coach in high school or college, and now do the majority of their training alone. Many are experiencing the joy of athletics for the first time, and don't know how hard a "hard" workout should feel or how easy an "easy" day should be. As a result, most push too hard on the easy days, which leaves them too tired to push hard enough on the hard days. It's exactly this type of athlete that can benefit most from a heart rate monitor.

What are They?

With each beat, the heart generates electrical signals that can be measured on the skin. A heart rate monitor transmitter contains two electrodes to detect these signals. The electrodes are mounted on a sealed transmitter that's attached to the chest with an elastic belt. The transmitter detects the voltage differential on the skin during every heart beat and relays the signal to a wrist receiver which displays heart rate in beats per minute.

Dr. Seppo "Say it Three Times Fast" Säynäjäkangas produced the first portable heart rate monitors in Finland in 1982, and by 1990 Polar was distributing a full line of inexpensive models to the US and world markets. Today, several manufacturers produce monitors for under $100, which makes them accessible even to recreational athletes.

Why Bother?

Let me say this one more time: The standard distances for most racewalkers range from 5km to 50km, so most of our energy requirements during races are met by aerobic as opposed to anaerobic metabolism. The bulk of our training for these races, then, needs to be easy aerobic distance work. Too much speed work, or too many hard miles on the roads will teach the muscles to rely on anaerobic glycolysis instead of aerobic metabolism, resulting in excess lactate production when racing. But most people tend to push too hard on their easy aerobic days without realizing it. A heart rate monitor can ensure that you're working aerobically throughout the workout.

Occasionally we do have to push ourselves in training, especially closer to racing season. But it can sometimes be difficult for us to maintain focus during hard tempo workouts and long threshold intervals. A heart rate monitor can help here too, pushing you when your legs and brain are telling you to slow down or stop.

Whether you're a beginner or an elite-level racewalker, you can benefit from a heart rate monitor's ability to keep you working at the right intensity level—in the right "target heart rate" (THR) zone—for any kind of workout: 65-75% of maximum heart rate on easy days, 70-75% on your long day, 80-85% for tempo workouts, about 85-92% for threshold intervals, and 95% and beyond for VO_2 max training. But how do you determine your maximum heart rate?

Finding Maximum Heart Rate

Studies have found that the average 20-year-old male college student has a maximum heart rate of 200 beats per minute, and that the average person's maximum heart rate declines by about 1 beat per minute per year. This leads to the simple formula:

$$\text{Maximum Heart Rate (MHR)} = 220 - \text{age}$$

The problem with the formula is that few people are "average"—especially athletes. If you've remained relatively fit since the age of 20, your maximum heart rate probably hasn't dropped very much at all. And women have, on average, maximum heart rates about 6 beats per minute higher than those of men. I've actually worked with a very fit 60-year-old woman who was able to routinely get her heart rate up to 240 beats per minute—80 beats per minute *higher* than her theoretical *maximum*. Clearly, the formula doesn't work for everyone.

To some degree, the Ball State formulas (below) are a more accurate alternative, but like the simple (220 – age) formula, they too ignore fitness:

$$\text{MHR for women} = 209 - [(0.7)\,(\text{age})]$$
$$\text{MHR for men} = 214 - [(0.8)\,(\text{age})]$$

The only truly accurate way to determine your maximum heart rate is to do something to push yourself to maximum. The problem here is in the doing: As you can probably imagine, it's not easy to push yourself to your absolute limit. You'll usually come pretty close at the end of a short race—1,500-meters or 1-mile—but only if you start out conservatively and really pour it on at the end. Otherwise, you'll rarely come to within ten beats of maximum in training, even during your hardest workouts.

The other tried-and-true approach is to do a maximum heart rate test under the supervision of a doctor or coach. This will usually entail starting out on a treadmill at about 5km-race speed, then increasing the elevation 1% at a time every minute until exhaustion. Another way is to do three or four all-out 400-meter repeats, with about a 1-minute rest between each, making sure to push absolutely as hard as you can the last 150 meters of the last repeat. If your racewalking technique isn't quite efficient enough to allow yourself to get up to a very high speed, you can do the test running.

But in any case, whichever way you do the test, remember I told you to do it under your doctor's supervision, right? So don't come cryin' to me when you keel over from a heart attack, okay? "Dave warned me":

Sign Here **X**...

The Karvonen Formula

Once you've determined your maximum heart rate, you could simply multiply your desired heart rate percentage by your maximum heart rate to find your target heart rate, but doing so doesn't take fitness into account. After you've been training a while your heart becomes larger and stronger. It can pump considerably more blood with each beat, so at rest and while exercising it has to beat fewer times per minute to pump the same amount of blood that it did when you were less fit.

The "average" person has a resting heart rate (RHR) of about 72 beats per minute, while a fit athlete may have a resting heart rate of less than 40 beats per minute. The Karvonen Formula takes these differences into account by first requiring you to find your Heart Rate Reserve (HRR)—the difference between your maximum heart rate and your resting heart rate.

Let's say I want to limit my heart rate to 75% of maximum on a long workout. This is my Target Heart Rate (THR). I found my Maximum

Heart Rate (MHR) to be about 197 beats per minute by doing a max heart rate treadmill test (under the supervision of the malpractice insurance-protected slide-rule jockeys at the Olympic Training Center). I found my Resting Heart Rate (RHR) to be 38 beats per minute by recording my heart rate every morning before getting out of bed. I use the Karvonen Formula to tell me how high I can let my heart rate drift during the workout:

$$\text{THR} = (\text{HRR x \% of intensity}) + \text{RHR, where HRR} = \text{MHR - RHR}$$
$$\text{THR} = ((197\text{-}38) \times .75) + 38$$
$$\text{THR} = 157.25$$

Even if you walk at a steady pace, your heart rate will generally rise throughout a long workout because heat builds up in the muscles, making enzymatic activity less efficient. Also, dehydration sets in, which thickens the blood, making it more difficult to pump. This gradual rise in heart rate is known as "heart rate drift," "cardiac drift," or "cardiac creep," and you need to take it into account when determining your training heart rate. Using the Karvonen formula, then, I know that I can't let my heart rate get any higher than 157 at any point during the workout. I also know that if I start out too close to that number, cardiac drift will push me over before long. So I'll start out with a heart rate in the 140s, and then let it rise to no higher than 157 beats per minute during the workout. If I get too close to my limit, I'll slow down.

How to Use a Heart Rate Monitor

Once you determine your maximum and target heart rates, there are a number of different ways you can use a heart rate monitor for training and racing:

1. As an equalizer. External factors such as heat, humidity, altitude and wind, and internal factors like dehydration, fatigue and psychological stress can profoundly affect your ability to perform. Ignoring these factors by attempting to train at a set pace per mile under difficult conditions can lead to overtraining. A heart rate monitor allows you to train at an even effort under any conditions.

2. As a governor. Sometimes it's hard to go easy. A monitor can ensure that LSD is long slow distance and recovery days are recovery days. It can also ensure that you don't go nuts in the first 400 meters of a race. There's no such thing as "free" energy: If you go out too hard at the start, it'll get you in the end.

3. As a butt-kicker. Sorry, but there are also days when you have to work really hard to get fitter. A heart rate monitor can ensure that you're sustaining an 85% effort on those tempo workouts, or 90 to 95% when doing hard intervals.

4. As a doctor. Keeping track of morning heart rate can give you forewarning if you're overtrained. If your resting heart rate is more than 10% higher than normal, it's time to back off: You're overtrained and probably on the verge of getting sick.

5. As a technique coach. By making slight changes to your technique while walking at a set pace on a treadmill, you can determine which variation is most efficient by watching for drops in heart rate.

Chapter 37: The Poop on Shoes

During the Q & A section of my clinics, someone will invariably ask, "What about shoes?" To which I'll respond, "I highly recommend them." For some reason they'll always want me to elaborate, so here are some things to remember when looking for something to keep the glass and nails from cutting up your feet when you walk:

1. Walking shoes are the worst possible things to wear for racewalking. By "Walking Shoes" I mean the big, stiff ugly ol' white leather "Nursing Shoes" the pimply faced kid in the mall will try to sell you when you tell him you're a racewalker. These things will cripple you if you try to racewalk in them. If you want to spend $69.99 or more for black toenails, blood blisters and shin splints, go ahead, but don't say I didn't warn you. A racewalking shoe should have:

2. Flexibility, both in the forefoot and medially. Frank Alongi used to say that you should be able to fold up a walking shoe and put it in your pocket like a wallet. Your shoe must be flexible enough to allow your feet to "roll" from heel to toe when you racewalk. If your shoe is too stiff to flex a bit from the middle of the shoe to the toe and a bit from side to side, you're going to be a very "stumpy" racewalker. And you'll probably end up with shin splints from your feet slapping down on the ground 200 times per minute instead of gracefully rolling along as they will in a more flexible pair of shoes.

3. A low heel. One of the many paradoxes of racewalking: The more cushioning you have in a shoe, the harder you'll hit the ground when you walk. Huh? It's like this: The foot acts like a lever, with the ankle as the fulcrum. The bigger the heel on the shoe, the more force you will have acting on this lever, forcing your foot to flatten out upon heel-strike. With a low heel your feet will roll very easily along the ground; with a "fat" heel your feet will hit the ground like a couple of sledgehammers.

4. A wide toe box. Make sure there's plenty of "wiggle room" for your feet to spread out. Cramped toes will become black and blistered toes.

5. Racewalking shoes, or running "racing flats" are the answer. If buying running shoes, look for something designed for racing 5kms to marathons, instead of sprint or cross-country flats, which may offer insufficient support. The shoes should be light-weight (6 1/2 to 9 ounces), low-profile and flexible, with a breathable upper.

6. Where? 90% of "Athletic Shoes" are bought by kids trying to look cool, so the vast majority of big-chain shoe stores don't sell anything for people who'll actually use them for athletic pursuits. Which is why racewalking shoes and running flats are so hard to find in the local shoe store. You'll probably have to resort to mail-order. Two of the best companies are Hoys, and Eastbay, both of which have web sites accessible under the "products" section of my web site (Appendix I). Or, if you're lucky enough to have a specialty running store in your area, have the manager special-order a pair of racing flats for you. That way you'll be sure to get the right shoe and the right fit.

7. Buy 'em big. If in doubt, buy shoes 1/2 size large rather than too small. Since you land on your heel, then roll forward when racewalking, your heel always stays pressed up against the back of the shoe—your foot won't slip as much as a runner's will, so you can get away with a shoe that's a bit large.

8. Goo 'em. The problem with racing flats is that the outsole usually wears out very quickly. But if your shoe is an "air" or "gel" model the midsole should stay firm through the next ice age. A tube of Shoe Goo, or glue from a hot glue gun will keep the outsole in shape for hundreds of miles. If you really like the shoes, you may even consider having them professionally re-soled (about $30).

Chapter 38: Care and Feeding of Racewalking Injuries

I'm still waiting for the tabloids to report on the <u>real</u> government cover up. Not the Elvis on Mars thing, or the pregnant crocodile-baby. I want them to expose The Big Lie: "Racewalking: the Injury-Free Sport!" What a crock! Show me a competitive racewalker who's been completely injury-free for more than a year or two, and I'll show you the photo I snapped of the Easter Bunny at the Krispy Kreme down on Main street. Racewalkers do receive substantially fewer injuries than runners, but to promote racewalking as an injury-free sport is a bit misleading.

I've been lucky enough over the years to train through most of my injuries. But I have had my fair share of nasties that have required medical attention, so I've seen a good number of doctors. Most sports medicine specialists get fine educations in our medical schools, and receive lots of great on-the-job training treating a daily throng of synchronized swimmers, horse shoe pitchers, dog mushers and limbo dancers. But the problem with doctors is that they work in generalities: If a doctor works with a lot of basketball players, a torn meniscus is probably a reasonable guess as the source of medial knee pain. Likewise, a sprain may be a likely diagnosis for a soccer player, and chondromalacia is fairly common among runners. Unfortunately most doctors have never seen a racewalker and aren't sure what kinds of assumptions they should make.

Origins and Insertions

I've found that racewalkers suffer relatively few serious injuries, but nearly all are overuse injuries rather than traumatic ones (i.e., sprains and tears). Tendonitis of the knee (iliotibial or sartorial), feet (plantar fasciitis or peroneal-cuboid syndrome), shins ("shin splints," anterior compartment syndrome or posterior tibial myositis/tendonitis), or of the Achilles tendon are all common overuse injuries in racewalkers. Bursitis of the hip or knee is also fairly common.

The trick with tendonitis is to remember just what tendons are: They're tough fibrous sheaths that connect muscles to bones. Fortunately, 99% of the time there's nothing wrong with the tendon itself—it's simply being abused by a tight muscle. As the muscle

184

shortens, it pulls at its origin and insertion points (at the tendons, and fascial sheaths).

Similarly, bursitis is the inflammation of a bursa (a fluid-filled sac found or formed in areas of friction). As the muscles tighten, friction around the joints increases and the bursae are irritated. The only way to release the strain on the tendon or bursa is to lengthen the muscle by stretching it. It's a lot like somebody pulling your hair: The hair itself doesn't hurt, it's the insertion point at the scalp that's making you scream. Anti-inflammatories, pain killers, ice, and thinking happy thoughts may all help, but eliminating that "pulling" is ultimately the only way to make it stop hurting.

The Quick Fix

Athletes are often seduced by a quick-fix, Band-Aid approach to sports medicine: Rest, ice and aspirin will make the pain go away. All true to some extent, but these approaches attack the symptom and not the cause. The pain may be in the tendon or bursa, but the root cause is the tight, neglected muscle.

Treatment for these injuries must begin with isolation of the muscle or muscles involved. In most cases the athlete will notice discomfort and tightness in muscles that may lie far from the injured area. Don't ignore these sensations! They could be the source of the irritation. My first serious bout with tendonitis involved the insertion of my iliotibial band into the outside of my right knee. I felt a little tightness on the outside of my right hip as well, but thought nothing of it, since it was never very painful and was so far away from the hurting knee.

The injury eventually forced me to take two months off, and to pull out of the '87 World Cup. Whenever I tried to return to training the knee would hurt just as much as it did at the time of the initial injury. Two months of rest did nothing to cure the knee because I failed to attack the tight hip muscles and iliotibial band. The treatment that finally cured me involved having a physical therapist dig at the "necrotic" scar tissue in my hip and thigh with the back end of a screwdriver to release the muscle and tendon, and then learning how to ward off further flare-ups with a sensible stretching routine.

An ounce of prevention is worth two in the bush (or something like that....) If the weather is just too lousy to get out the door to train, stay inside and stretch! Attack those tight muscles before they turn into debilitating injuries.

Rehabilitation

Certainly stretching is an important first step in recovery, but gains in flexibility will be short-lived if the involved muscles are weak and atrophied. Strength training is equally critical in injury rehabilitation or preventative care. Whether using free weights, weight machines, elastic devices or isometric exercises, the involved muscles should be isolated in such a way as to ensure that they are being worked through a range of motion that mimics the racewalking action as closely as possible. This may involve a good deal of improvisation with weight machines, or experimentation with postural changes until the perfect position is found.

During rehabilitation, resistance should be just enough to cause minor fatigue without causing pain in the injured area. As strength improves, work up to three sets of 10-12 RM. Always allow 48 hours for recovery between sessions—three days of weight training per week is optimum.

A SCARIER Method of Injury Treatment

Although the RICE method—Rest, Ice, Compression, Elevation—is somewhat effective in treating racewalking injuries, it leaves out a few important elements: Stretching, Rehydration and Anti-inflammatories. Racewalkers with injuries shouldn't stop at RICE, but should try something SCARIER: Stretch, Compress, Anti-inflammatories, Rehydrate, Ice, Elevate, Rest.

> **Stretch** the muscles. Most racewalking injuries are tendonitis or bursitis-type injuries. The root cause of these injuries is tight muscles that "pull" on tendon insertions. Stretching the tight muscles will relieve the strain on the tendon insertions.
>
> **Compress** the sore spots to push out excess fluids. Also "compress"—by massaging—the tight muscles to work out any knots, and to break up scar tissue.
>
> **Anti-inflammatories** like ibuprofen (Advil) or Aleve will further reduce swelling.

186

Rehydrate those dried out, beef-jerky muscles. Muscles are 90% water—a dry muscle is a tight muscle. DRINK!

Ice 10 minutes on, 10 minutes off for 30 minutes, after training.

Elevate the feet whenever possible. Elevation will allow fluid to drain out of the swollen spots—just try to keep your feet out of your food if you put them up on the dinner table.

Rest as a last resort. If at all possible, continue walking, but take it easy. Warming up the muscles will allow you to get a better stretch, and will circulate lots of healing blood to the area. I don't think of it as "training," but as "therapeutic walking."

While tendonitis-type injuries are the most "serious" injuries that a racewalker is likely to suffer, there are a number of minor inconveniences that may befall you. You should be able to take care of these minor problems easily, without missing any training. Among these are:

1. Blisters. Blisters form in places where the skin is rubbed repeatedly, usually by an ill-fitting shoe. Many walkers have found that rubbing Vaseline on their feet before training will prevent blisters. This is definitely a case of the cure being worse than the ailment—see #4 for more on the subject. Runners generally find relief by wearing double-layered socks. But since our feet don't tend to move around in our shoes as much as a runner's foot does, these socks may actually *cause* blister problems because they allow the foot to slide around more than they would in a single-thickness pair of socks. Experiment with different sock thicknesses to see what works best for you, and never go out on a long workout in a pair of shoes or socks that you haven't tested first on several shorter workouts. If you already have a blister, I say pop it with a sterilized needle, then cover it with a Band-Aid or sterile gauze, although Ms. Kennedy, my old high school nurse, is apt to be very upset when she reads this. I find that if I don't drain the fluid, the blister eventually tears open and then things get *really* ugly. Eventually, frequently blistered areas will thicken, forming a hard, scaly callous—so at least you have that to look forward to.

2. Black toenails. Formed when blood collects in a blister under a traumatized toenail, these ugly buggers will really impress your friends. Although black toenails are most frequently caused by tight shoes, they can also form when your shoes are too large, so you're damned if you do, and damned if you don't. The nail will eventually "die" and fall off, but if it really hurts you may want to see a podiatrist who'll pop a hole in the nail with a hot paper clip—a high-tech solution I now do myself for about 85 bucks less than the D.P.M. version. Keeping your toenails clipped will help prevent them from recurring.

3. Side stitches. Not an injury, *per se,* but they can be pretty painful, nonetheless. A side stitch is a temporary pain in the side, below or under the rib cage, caused by an insufficient oxygen supply to the diaphragm—a muscle sheath below the lungs that helps you breath. If you get a stitch while training, bend sideways away from the side that hurts, while massaging the area. The theory behind the cure is that you're trying to get oxygen into the area—although simply stopping your walk to do the stretch will probably do as much good as the stretch itself. Eventually, as you get fitter, oxygen supply to the diaphragm increases and the stitches stop occurring.

4. Chafing. Chafing is a nasty rash that occurs when you rub two pieces of skin together about 200 times per minute. It most commonly occurs when you're dehydrated—after you've stopped sweating and your skin is left covered with a film of sticky salt. Staying hydrated will help, as will wearing half-tights under your shorts—in the case of thigh chafing anyway. Losing weight will also help—enough said. Many walkers solve the problem by smearing the affected areas with Vaseline before training and racing, but I'm having a hard time imagining anything more awful than that fate. I'm not afraid of snakes, spiders, or rabid Rotweilers, but Vaseline? Now that stuff gives me the willies!

Coming Back From an Injury

Patience is the keyword when returning from an injury—don't rush things. Again, most walking injuries are *overuse* injuries. Your body is trying to tell you something: "Take it easy, Dummy!"

A certain amount of detraining will set in after any layoff; speed is the first thing to go, but before long endurance is also degraded. The good news is that it takes a lot less time to return to top form than it took to get there in the first place, so don't rush it.

I've often been told that it takes two weeks to come back from every week off, but I've found that it seems to take two weeks to return from *any* layoff. If I've been off for a month, the first two weeks back will feel like garbage, but then things will always "click" suddenly after about two weeks. One rule of thumb that I do believe, however, is that you shouldn't race after a layoff until you've gotten at least as much training in as you've lost. If you were off for two weeks, don't even think about racing unless you've gotten at least two good weeks under your belt after the break. If you were off for six weeks, get in six weeks of training before racing.

Although injuries may be an inevitable part of racewalk training, if you know how to treat them, your down time will be measured in days rather than weeks or months.

Michelle Rohl on:
Returning to Training After a Layoff

Accomplishments: 1992, 1996 and 2000 Olympian. Top U.S. finisher in all three Olympic Games, and winner of the 2000 Olympic Trials. 15th at the 1995 IAAF World Track & Field Championships 10km walk. American record-holder for the outdoor track 5km (20:56) and 10km (44:41), and the outdoor road 10km (44:06) and 20km (1:31:51).

Personal Records:
3 kilometers: 12:27
5 kilometers: 20:56
10 kilometers: 44:06
20 kilometers: 1:31:51

Background: Michelle was a 15-time NAIA track and cross-country All-American, and the 1987 NAIA indoor 1,000-meter and 2-mile champion. After competing in the 1,500-meter run at the 1988 USA Track & Field nationals, Michelle decided to try to qualify for 1989 nationals in the 10km walk when she missed the qualifying standard in the 1,500-meter run. She qualified, placed 10th, then was 6th at the U.S. Olympic Festival one month later.

A mother of three, Michelle has learned a lot about returning from training layoffs: After the birth of her first child, Molly, in July of 1990, Michelle suffered a series of medical problems when she returned to training too quickly. Michelle gave herself more time after son Sebastian was born in May 1993, and went on to break the American record for the 10km racewalk at the 1994 Goodwill Games. After giving birth to daughter Ayla, in August of 1997, Michelle discussed her strategy for returning to training:

Michelle Says: "Since all three of my children were born in late spring or summer, I've always run cross-country to get back into shape after the layoff. I started training only two weeks after Molly was born, but that turned out to be a bad idea. After Sebastian I decided to take things a little more conservatively and had better results. For the first two or three weeks I did some swimming and biking, then I slowly started adding in some running and racewalking.

"I learned to not do anything competitive after a break in training until I'm really in shape. The technique isn't there and I lose a lot of strength, especially the strength to do hills. I find that running cross-country and lifting weights really helps. I even try to do some lifting during the pregnancy. When I'm ready to start running and walking again, I find that some days it feels better to run, some days it feels better to walk; I just take it slow and do whatever feels better.

"If I can't walk for at least 15 minutes, It's not worth the bother, so I'll go back to swimming and riding the stationary bike for a while. The longer I've taken off, the longer I'll give myself to get back into racing or intense training. That's the most important thing to remember after any break in training: You need to be really patient, and give your body as long as it needs to recover fully and regain most of your strength and endurance."

Chapter 39: Preventing Dog Attacks

Nothing puts a damper on a good workout like losing a leg to a Pit Bull. But although common sense can prevent most attacks, since dogs are not "natural" creatures—we've selectively in-bred them to the point of comical excess (Ever seen a Chihuahua try to "get friendly" with a great Dane's hind leg?)—they're apt to behave in somewhat bizarre and unpredictable ways. In any case, there are a few things you should definitely NOT do when confronted by a Kamikaze canine charging at you like Dennis Rodman on crack. Among these:

The Don'ts

> **1.) Ignore the owner.** Do NOT pay attention to anything the owner says or does—this is between you and the crazed beast—the dog, that is. I once lost a good-sized chunk of hip flesh to a German Shepherd who's owner assured me that "Princess" wouldn't bite— that she was just "playing." Playing, in this case, meaning locking on to a terrified 12-year-old's hip and shaking vigorously until beaten off with a flurry of fists, feet, elbows and knees. It may be embarrassing for you to beat a dog senseless while the owner stands by with mouth agape, but Zen-like focus on the task at hand has kept me bite-free ever since.

> **2.) Face the music.** Never "Play Dead" or turn your back on a dog. Unlike bears, who'll just swat you around a bit like they do in the old Bugs Bunny cartoons, the typical genetically scrambled mutt will only become confused by such behaviors and mistake you for a giant, cowering salami.

> **3.) You ain't no rabbit.** If it's just you against Fido, never ever try to outrun the dog. I'd put my money on a blind, three-legged Pekinese against Michael Johnson every time. ANY dog can outrun ANY human any day

of the week. Research has shown that to 43% of unchained dogs, a brightly colored pair of rapidly departing running shorts is indistinguishable from a rapidly departing Frisbee, and will elicit an identical "Jump and Chomp" response; 34% will mistake you for a flying two-legged salami; while the remaining 23% will be asleep on the porch—no doubt dreaming about chewing on your leg like an old soup bone.

I could probably go on forever here: Never go running or walking with your cat on a leash; never use Alpo in the place of Vaseline as a pre-workout lubricant; never exercise with pork chops in your pockets.... But it's probably more beneficial for most people to know what they *should* do if they're ever confronted by that deranged Doberman down the block.

Now don't quote me on this stuff: I'm not an AKC-Certified Dog Wrangler—although I do play one on television. But the following are some things that have worked for me in the past—proven strategies that may help you to remain bipedal for many years to come... Probably... Well, maybe... If you're real lucky... And you keep clear of the house at the end of my street where the two Satanic Labradors live—the ones who ate the UPS driver last week....

And the Dos

1.) Be the Top Dog. When a Menacing mongrel comes bolting at you with fur and fangs flying, run directly at the dog, yelling maniacally and waving your arms like Jack Nicholson escaping from a straight jacket. These belligerent beasts are used to being the aggressors. When they see that you are bigger, louder and more serious than they are, they'll usually back down. (Amazing but true: We've so screwed up dogs' natural instincts that they actually take Jack Nicholson seriously.)

2.) Every man for himself. If and only if you're with training partners, use them as human shields/sacrificial lambs and run like Gilligan when his pants catch on fire at the end of the "Dinner with the Head-Hunters" episode. Your mantra should be, "I don't have to outrun the dog, I just have to outrun my friends."

3.) Smash 'em! If you have enough time, grab a good Goliath-slaying-sized rock or a hefty stick, and try your best to merge it at high velocity with the dog's frontal lobe; where the "kill" impulse originates. It's amazing how quickly this will communicate the message that you do not wish to become his rawhide chew toy at any time during that particular workout. Even if you miss (and you're real lucky) you may be able to trigger the bonehead's human-induced "fetch" response, instantly transforming the evil cur into a tail-wagging, spit-slobbering Pavlovian marshmallow.

4.) Try "The Poitras." I wouldn't recommend it, but if you have The Gift you may want to try "The Poitras": I was working out on a country road with Canadian Olympian, Tina Poitras, and two of my U.S. Team training partners in LaGrange one day in 1996, when we were suddenly charged by an enraged Rotweiler. I was ready to employ strategy #1, Ernesto* looked like he was going for #3, while Wolfgang* looked like a deer caught in the headlights, ready to try the Wet-My-Pants-&-Hope-the-Doggie-Stops-to-Sniff-the-Puddle Method. Tina, instead, simply held out her hand and began cooing "Good boy! What a good doggie you are!" in her soothing French-Canadian accent. Amazing stuff at work here, folks: the brute stopped instantly to let himself be scratched and stroked while we stood and watched in amazement. Even Wolfgang was ready to roll onto his back for a good belly rub.

5.) Pepper spray. Finally, as a last resort, mace the little &@$+@&% to Kingdom Come. It didn't work for the UPS guy, but he did have his hands full at the time with those 40 lb. crates from the Salami of the Month Club....

---

*Note: Some names have been changed to protect the timid.

Chapter 40: Recruiting Good Potential Racewalkers

Success in racewalking requires a unique combination of athletic endowments unlike that of any other sport. U.S. coaches have traditionally steered unsuccessful distance runners towards the walks by default. Our European and "South of the Border" counterparts, however, are very methodical in selecting athletes for the racewalks.

Very young athletes in the former "Iron Curtain" countries underwent rigorous testing to determine their potential in various athletic pursuits. Tests of speed, strength and flexibility showed coaches which athletes were potential Olympic Medal-winning racewalkers. After selection, the racewalkers received the same treatment from the government supported "Sports Machine" as the runners and other athletes. A similar approach has been very successful in selecting potential world-class racewalkers in Australia.

Mexico, a dominant force in racewalking since the 1960s, actively recruits the most talented young athletes in the country to become racewalkers. The Escuela Mexicana de Caminata or the "Mexican Racewalk School" has been established by the Mexican Sports Federation to recruit and train the best of these young athletes. Children between the ages of 11 and 17 undergo rigorous physical aptitude tests and medical exams for selection to the school. Accepted athletes receive free room and board at La Instituto Estatal de la Juventud y el Deporte— the State Institute of youth Sports. The most successful of these athletes are invited to train at the CDOM, the Mexican Olympic Training Center, where they receive top coaching, free room and board, and monetary stipends.

To compete with such systems we must more actively recruit talented young athletes to participate in racewalking. But what constitutes a good potential racewalker? In general, successful racewalkers must be blessed with:

> **1. Flexibility.** Racewalkers need sufficient knee flexibility to allow straightening of the leg in the single-support phase, and hip-flexor and ankle flexibility to enable a long effective stride length.

2. Coordination. You don't necessarily have to be able to juggle chainsaws, but a certain degree of bilateral coordination is necessary to keep those arms and legs moving efficiently.

3. Good fundamental speed. 100-meter speed for example. You don't need to be a great sprinter to be a great racewalker, but if you don't have at least some basic speed you'll have a hard time attaining the high stride frequencies that racewalking demands.

4. Excellent "speed endurance." 800-meter speed is a good test of an athlete's ability to *maintain* these quick turnover rates. The ability to maintain a rapid turnover is even more important than top speed.

5. An ectomorph or mesomorph body type. 6'4"/240 lbs. is *not* the ideal body type for racewalkers.

Obviously then, unsuccessful distance runners are not logical candidates as potential racewalkers. Not only do top-notch racewalkers require the same physiological determinants that excellent runners possess, they must also possess a high degree of neuromuscular coordination to excel in the sport.

Does this mean you should forget about racewalking if you don't live up to these criteria? Certainly not! Desire and hard work are *at least* as important as the physical determinants of racewalking success. In fact, I know a number of 6'4"/240 lb. racewalkers who can probably kick your butt all over the track. But they're not walking to make the next Olympic team, they just want to see how fast they can make *their* bodies go.

Racewalking is a great sport for anyone wanting to test their limits: The mix of technique, speed and endurance presents a challenge to anyone, regardless of their natural "gifts"—whether they're potential stars or not. If you enjoy racewalking, train and train hard. If you work at it, you <u>will</u> succeed!

Chapter 41: Racewalking for Runners

In a former life I was a runner. I did all the running stuff: I bought the shoes, read the magazines, ran the races, and even trained about 45 miles per week. For my dedication I ran times in the mid-17s for 5km, and just under 5:00 for the mile.

These days I'm perfectly content zipping through life as a racewalker, but occasionally I get a wild hair and jump into a local running race—just to see what'll happen. What usually happens is I run in the mid-17s for 5km, and just under 5:00 for the mile. No better or worse than in high school, but at least now I don't waste my time with that 45 miles per week of running training.

Now don't get me wrong; I treat the race just as seriously as everyone else toeing the line. I'll wear my favorite shorts and racing singlet. I'll lace up my best racing flats and partake in the same pre-race rituals as the other runners. I just don't bother doing any more than about 2 1/2 miles of easy jogging per week—about 500 meters at a time—as part of my daily pre-racewalking warm-up.

Must Be the Walkin'

How, then, can I run times that will put me in the top ten of most local "fun runs?" "Natural" ability? Hardly. Youthful energy? Please. I'm 32, for crying out loud. What then? Most hard-core runners don't want to hear it, but it's the walking, folks. And I'm certainly not alone. Michelle Rohl, American record-holder in the women's 10km racewalk, not only made the '92 and '96 Olympic teams as a racewalker, she also qualified for the 1996 Olympic *marathon* trials. Michelle never qualified for the Olympic Trials as a runner when she was solely focusing on her running training, yet she managed to do it while devoting most of her weekly miles to her racewalk training. Debbi Lawrence, another convert to racewalking, ran national-class times while injured and doing nothing but racewalk training for months at a time.

All the Benefits of Running...

Seems worthy of a little investigating, now doesn't it? The empirical evidence is convincing enough for me, but the techies at the U.S. Olympic Training Center in Colorado Springs were curious enough to want some hard data. So we gave it to them: Jay Kearney, a physiologist at the Training Center, compared VO_2 max values for 15 U.S. National Racewalk Team members, and 10 Mexican National Team members both while racewalking and running. The study concluded that *"these athletes are capable of achieving similar VO_2 max values for racewalking and running, which indicates a potential cross-training effect."*

At the time of the study I didn't do any running training, and I've spent plenty of time at the CDOM—the Mexican Olympic Training Center—and found that the Mexicans don't do any running training either. Yet, some of us had VO_2 max values in the high 70s. That is, *racewalkers* were able to take in and process nearly 80 milliliters of oxygen per kilogram of body mass per minute both while racewalking *and* while running—even though most of us did no running training before the treadmill tests. For comparison, Frank Shorter had a VO_2 max of "only" 71.3 in 1972 when he won the Olympic Marathon. He shouldn't feel bad though, poor Frank never learned to racewalk....

...Without the Injuries

Clearly, racewalking is an unparalleled aerobic conditioner, yet it's much easier on the body than running. Over the years I've taught dozens of injured runners to racewalk so they could train through their running injuries. By cutting back on their running mileage—and making up the difference with quality racewalking workouts—these runners have remained injury-free and have improved their running times dramatically. Many have come back to me with stories of big personal records after weeks, or even months of sharply reduced running training. I've also taught several ultra-marathoners to racewalk so they would have an advantage over their unenlightened competitors who must inevitably walk for long stretches during their six-day runs. Again, huge personal records.

Crossover Training

It wouldn't be a stretch to say that racewalking is by far the best substitute activity for injured runners. But why wait for an injury? It's more than just very good *cross-training*, racewalking is unparalleled *crossover* training. The two are similar enough so that training for one will give very good results in the other. This isn't the case with most other sports. Triathletes don't just train on their bikes—they need to swim and run as well, because the individual events are so different there is very little crossover between them.

Racewalking appears unique in that runners don't seem to have to do much "re-wiring" to convert their racewalking fitness to running fitness. Add to that the reduced chance of injury, and you have the "Holy Grail" that runners have been searching for—a supplemental, low-impact exercise that can directly improve their running performances.

Debbi Lawrence on:

Making the Transition from Runner to Racewalker

Accomplishments: 1992, '96 and '00 Olympian. Winner of the '88 (exhibition), '92 and '96 Olympic Racewalk Trials. Winner of ten outdoor and four indoor national championships, and American record holder for the 5 kilometer (road) racewalk, and the indoor track 1,500-meter, 1-mile, and 3 kilometer racewalks.

Personal Records:
1,500 meters:	5:53
1 mile:	6:16
3 kilometers:	12:20
5 kilometers:	21:15
10 kilometers:	44:42
20 kilometers:	1:33:48

Background: Debbi was a 15-time All-American in cross-country and track while running for the University of Wisconsin at Parkside. Despite frequent debilitating injuries, she won the NAIA indoor mile and outdoor 1,500-meter runs, and was the National Junior College indoor 2-mile champion while competing for Gateway Technical College. She began racewalking as a way to stay fit when injuries prevented her from running.

Debbi Says: "I hated making the transition from running to racewalking, because I had always been a runner and I continued to be a runner in my mind. I only racewalked because my coach [U. Wisconsin-Parkside coach, Mike DeWitt] made me do it whenever I was injured and couldn't run. At first, I racewalked a few weeks at a time as cross-training, but the running injuries seemed to take longer and longer to heal as the years went by, so I began to racewalk more and more. I made my first international racewalk team in 1982, but I went to Norway for the race thinking that I didn't belong there.

"Racewalking hurt a lot at first. I had developed a lot of fitness from running for so many years, but the walking muscles really weren't developed yet. I'd be able to walk pretty fast in my workouts and races, but I was always so sore the next day I'd hardly be able to move. I was always really happy when my running was going well and I was injury-

200

free, but those periods got shorter and shorter every year. I was usually able to get through the cross-country seasons, but as soon as track season started I would wind up re-injuring myself. In fact, I was hurt the entire spring season of 1983—I didn't run a step for the three months leading up to NAIA nationals. I jogged a few miles in the week before the meet, just to learn how to run again, but otherwise I was doing nothing but racewalk training all season. Still, I somehow wound up placing 3rd in the 3,000-meter run. I was really motivated to start running again after that, but then I earned a spot on the U.S. team being sent to Swedish Walk Week, so I continued to racewalk for the rest of the summer. My times improved dramatically, but I remember being very relieved when cross-country season finally rolled around.

"I continued making international teams every year, and I was actually making some money from racewalking, so there was just enough motivation to keep me going. But I don't think I really saw myself as a racewalker until at least 1988. That year I won the women's exhibition racewalk at the U.S. Olympic Trials, and then placed third in the Pan Am Cup against some of the best walkers in the world. Since then I've really learned to love the sport.

"I think my biggest problem early on was that I tried whatever anybody told me about racewalking technique or training, no matter what the source. After every race, a well-meaning judge, coach or athlete would give me a new bit of advice. It seemed like I was trying a different technique almost every week, so I always felt really stiff. Looking back, I think I just never gave my technique a chance to gel. I tried to do everything anyone ever told me, so the technique never really clicked. I think a beginning walker should seek out a coach—find a source of good advice and stick with it until things come together."

CONCLUSION

By taking the time to read this book you've proven your commitment to the most versatile form of exercise there is: racewalking. By using proper racewalking form, cardiac patients can exercise gently without fear of injury or over-stress, dieters can exercise to lose weight, and competitive athletes can set their sights on local road race or Olympic glory.

Wherever you are in your racewalking career, the techniques presented in the preceding chapters will help you to achieve your goals. But having this knowledge is only the first step. Now it's time to get out and do the work; the technique work, the physical training and the psychological preparation that you'll need to break down those barriers to efficient technique and fast times.

I'll continue to do the same myself, so maybe some day soon I'll see you "at the races." Be sure to come up and say hello!

APPENDIX I:

THINGS TO DO WHEN YOU'RE NOT RACEWALKING

There are a number of things you can do and places you can go to "stay connected" when you're not busy walking. Here are a few suggestions:

Buy shoes. Very few local shoe stores sell anything resembling racewalking shoes. Most walkers resort to buying from catalogues. The following outfits sell excellent running "racing flats" as well as real live racewalking shoes, often at discounted prices:

Sports 'N More: **(800) 397-5480**
Eastbay: **(800) 826-2205**   **www.eastbay.com**
Road Runner Sports: **(800) 551-5558**   **www.roadrunnersports.com**

Get on-line. There is a group of about 500 racewalkers worldwide hooked up to a racewalking interest group. You'll find race schedules and results, experts to answer your racewalking-related questions, and reams of mindless chatter. Sign up by sending a blank e-mail message to:

Subscribe-racewalking@yahoogroups.com

When you want to send a message to the group, send an e-mail to:

Racewalking@yahoogroups.com

The marathonwalkers group is a great source of support if you're interested in walking marathons and 50Ks. Sign up by sending a blank e-mail message to:

Subscribe-marathonwalkers@yahoogroups.com

When you want to send a message to the group, send an e-mail to:

Marathonwalkers@yahoogroups.com

Surf the Web. There are a growing number of racewalking web sites. My site, Dave's World Class Racewalking, has clinic information, articles, an elite athlete photo gallery and links to lots of other walking-related sites. The address is:

www.racewalking.org

Read all about it: The Ohio Racewalker is a real "underground" publication, but very informative. It's a steal at $10 per year (12 issues). Race calendar, results and articles about racewalking can be had by sending $10 to Jack Mortland at:

Ohio Racewalker   3184 Summit Street   Columbus, OH 43202

APPENDIX II:

ADDITIONAL RESOURCES

In addition to the Magazines and on-line sources listed in Appendix I, there are a number of other ways to find coaching, learn more about competitions and racewalking clubs in your area or to find out how to start your own club. Among these are:

Dave's World Class Racewalking

I conduct one or two week-long racewalking camps and 15-18 weekend clinics per year in cities throughout the U.S. For a clinic schedule or information on how to host a clinic in your hometown, visit the clinic information board on my World Class website at:

www.racewalking.org

North American Race Walking Foundation (NARWF)

Elaine Ward's organization was founded in 1986 to promote Racewalking in the United States and Canada. The Foundation provides information on how to find a club or coach, how to start a club, how to become a certified racewalk judge, and just about anything else related to the sport. The organization also sells a number of books and videos on technique and training. For further information, call or fax **(818) 577-2264**, e-mail **NARWF@aol.com** or write to:

NARWF
P.O. Box 50312
Pasadena, CA 91115-0312

Walkers Club of America

Founded in 1911, the WCA is the oldest active walking club in the U.S. The club promotes walking for competition and exercise, and offers quarterly newsletters, instructor certification, walking training camps, and assistance in starting your own club.

Howard Jacobson, Executive Director
Walkers Club of America
33 Saddle Lane
Levittown, NY 11756

Leukemia Society of America's Team in Training Program

Have you ever wanted to walk a marathon? Team in Training is the largest marathon training program in the country. You'll be provided with a qualified coach who will train you to go the distance, training partners for weekly group workouts, and an all-expense-paid trip to a marathon in exotic locales like Anchorage, Bermuda, Honolulu or London, in exchange for helping to raise money for the Leukemia Society.

For information on a chapter in your area call:

(800) 482-TEAM

or visit their web site at:

www.lsa-teamintraining.org

USA Track & Field (USATF)

USATF is the national governing body for track and field, cross-country, long-distance running, and racewalking. The organization supports youth, junior, senior and masters programs and competitions throughout the U.S., and is a good source of information on the Junior Olympic and World Veterans organizations. For information on the chapter in your area, contact the national office at:

USA Track & Field
One RCA Dome, Suite 140
Indianapolis, IN 46225
(317) 261-0500

APPENDIX III:

Kilometer to Mile Conversions

The vast majority of racewalking races—including all championship races—are contested in metric distances. The Olympic distances are 10km, 20km, 50km, and most local races are 5kms and 10kms. You should get used to thinking in terms of kilometers instead of miles when training, so you'll understand your splits on a standard 2km racing loop, or on a standard 400-meter track. (Most tracks are 400 meters, <u>not</u> 1/4 mile, so four laps is 1,600 meters, whereas a mile is 1,609.1 meters.) The following conversions will help you to make the transition:

Pace per km	Pace per mile	Pace per km	Pace per mile
4:00	6:26	5:00	8:03
4:05	6:34	5:05	8:11
4:10	6:42	5:10	8:19
4:15	6:50	5:15	8:27
4:20	6:58	5:20	8:35
4:25	7:06	5:25	8:43
4:30	7:14	5:30	8:51
4:35	7:23	5:35	8:59
4:40	7:31	5:40	9:07
4:45	7:39	5:45	9:15
4:50	7:47	5:50	9:23
4:55	7:55	5:55	9:31

Kilometer to Mile Conversions

Pace per km	Pace per mile	Pace per km	Pace per mile
6:00	9:39	8:00	12:52
6:05	9:47	8:05	13:00
6:10	9:55	8:10	13:08
6:15	10:03	8:15	13:17
6:20	10:11	8:20	13:25
6:25	10:19	8:25	13:33
6:30	10:28	8:30	13:41
6:35	10:36	8:35	13:49
6:40	10:44	8:40	13:57
6:45	10:52	8:45	14:05
6:50	11:00	8:50	14:13
6:55	11:08	8:55	14:21
7:00	11:16	9:00	14:29
7:05	11:24	9:05	14:37
7:10	11:32	9:10	14:45
7:15	11:40	9:15	14:53
7:20	11:48	9:20	15:01
7:25	11:56	9:25	15:09
7:30	12:04	9:30	15:17
7:35	12:12	9:35	15:25
7:40	12:20	9:40	15:33
7:45	12:28	9:45	15:41
7:50	12:36	9:50	15:49
7:55	12:44	9:55	15:57

APPENDIX IV:

TRAINING SCHEDULES FOR VARIOUS DISTANCES

Dang! I was hoping you wouldn't find this section! Like I said in the introduction to section II, I don't like writing detailed training schedules unless I can get frequent feedback from the athlete. But I also realize that most people don't have a coach, so they need something on paper to follow; some kind of guidance to assure them that they're headed in the right direction.

The physiological principles behind any training program are the same, but there are many ways to skin a banana: The following schedules are to be taken as suggestions or models, not The Law. These are typical schedules for the end of the base building, threshold and taper phases.

Don't jump right into things—make the transition from your present situation to the base schedule slowly. If you have time for a four-month base period, take your time working up to the prescribed distances then maintain, letting your pace increase as you get fitter. Then progress through the threshold and taper phases as described in chapters 10 and 12—schedule a taper for one or two weeks before your goal race, then a four to six week threshold phase before that, then a nice long base period before that.

It's okay to substitute an "easy" 5km or 10km race for one of the Saturday or Sunday workouts, but don't fall into the trap of skipping your long day every weekend so you can race. If you must race frequently, shift your days around so the race replaces your tempo workouts or, in a pinch, do a long warm up and cool down before and after the race or some extra distance later in the day—after a nap of course!

Finally, all workouts except for very easy days should be preceeded by a 10- to 20-minute warm up of easy racewalking or jogging then racewalking, followed by several minutes of dynamic flexibility drills. Do not omit this warm up! If time is limited, it's better to do the warm up and drills and cut the workout short than to do the whole workout without warming up fully. The schedules:

5km Training Schedule

Day	Base-Building	Threshold	Taper
M	Off	Off	Off
T	Economy: 10-12 x 200 meters fast with easy 200-meter rests or 3-4 x (100, 200, 300) fast with 100-meter rests	10 x 400 meters @ 5 seconds faster than 5km goal pace, with 1:00 rests between each	1/2 Economy: 6 x 200 meters or 5 x 400 meters with 200-meter recoveries
W	Easy 8-10 kilometers	Easy 45 minutes	Easy 30 minutes
T	Off or easy 30-45 minutes walking or cross training	Tempo walk: 10-20-10 or 4-6km acceleration tempo on alternate weeks	Tempo: Easy 10 minutes, fast 10 minutes, easy 10 minutes
F	Tempo: 10 minutes easy, 20 fast, 10 easy one week, and a 4-6km acceleration tempo the alternate week	Off or easy 30-45 minutes	Easy 20 minutes
S	Easy 30-45 minutes	5 x 1km @ 5km goal pace with 2:00 rests between each	Easy 20 mins. warm up plus dynamic flexibility drills, then 4 x 30 secs. fast, then stretch
S	15 kilometers at 70-75% of MHR	15 kilometers at 70-75% of MHR	Personal Record 5km Race!

10km Training Schedule

Day	Base-Building	Threshold	Taper
M	Off	Off	Off
T	Economy: 10-12 x 200 meters fast with easy 200-meter rests or 3-4 x (100, 200, 300) fast with 100-meter rests	20 x 400 meters @ 5 seconds faster than 10km goal pace, with 1:00 rests between each	1/2 Economy: 6 x 200 meters or 10 x 400 meters with 200-meter recoveries
W	Easy 15 kilometers	Easy 45 minutes	Easy 30 minutes
T	Off or easy 30-45 minutes walking or cross training	Tempo walk: 10-40-10 or 8-12 km acceleration tempo on alternate weeks	Tempo: Easy 10 minutes, fast 10 minutes, easy 10 minutes
F	Tempo: 10 minutes easy, 40 minutes fast, 10 minutes easy one week, and an 8-10 km acceleration tempo the alternate week	Off or easy 30-45 minutes	Easy 20 minutes
S	Easy 30-45 minutes	8 x 1km or 3 x 2km @ 10km goal pace with 2:00 rests between each	Easy 20 mins. warm up plus flexibility drills, then 4 x 30 seconds fast, then stretch
S	20 kilometers at 70-75% of MHR	20 kilometers at 70-75% of MHR	Personal Record 10km Race!

20km Training Schedule

Day	Base-Building	Threshold	Taper
M	Off	Off	Off
T	Economy: 10-12 x 200 meters fast with easy 200-meter rests or 3-4 x (100, 200, 300) fast with 100-meter rests	20-40 x 400 meters @ 5 seconds faster than 20km goal pace, with 1:00 rests between each	1/2 Economy: 6 x 200 meters or 4 x 400 meters with 200-meter rests
W	Easy 15-25 kilometers	Easy 45 minutes	Easy 30 minutes
T	Off or easy 30-45 minutes walking or cross training	Tempo walk: 16-20km steady-state or acceleration tempo on alternate weeks	Tempo: Easy 10 minutes, fast 10 minutes, easy 10 minutes
F	Tempo: 16-20km steady-state or acceleration tempo the alternate week	Off or easy 30-45 minutes	Easy 20 minutes
S	Easy 30-45 minutes	8-12 x 1km or 5-6 x 2km @ 20km goal pace with 2:00 rests between each	Easy 20 mins. warm up, plus flexibility drills, then 4 x 30 seconds fast, then stretch
S	30 kilometers at 70-75% of MHR	20-30 kilometers at 70-75% of MHR	Personal Record 20km Race!

GLOSSARY

Aerobic metabolism The creation of energy through the combustion of carbohydrates and fats in the presence of oxygen.

Anaerobic metabolism The creation of energy through the combustion of carbohydrates in the absence of oxygen.

Cardiac drift The tendency for heart rate to rise gradually throughout a workout due to dehydration and rising temperature within the muscles.

Center of gravity An imaginary point that would exist if you crushed your body down to a single, centrally located point. In humans, this point lies behind, and just below, the navel.

Creeping Racewalking without straightening the knee from the moment of heel contact to the vertical support phase.

Cross-training Training in activities other than racewalking, to improve fitness without over-taxing the racewalking muscles.

DQ Also, disqualification or "Dairy Queen." Occurs when three judges decide that your walking technique does not conform to the rules of racewalking: you are "lifting" or "creeping."

Double-support phase The brief part of a racewalker's stride when both feet are in contact with the ground.

Driving phase The component of a racewalker's stride that occurs between the point when the back foot leaves the ground, and when the heel of that foot makes contact with the ground in front of the body.

Economy A measure of how efficiently an athlete utilizes oxygen when exercising. An economical racewalker is able to walk fast while working at a relatively low percentage of his or her VO_2 max

Economy repeats Bursts of short, fast racewalking, interspersed with long rest intervals. Economy repeats teach a racewalker to walk efficiently at high speed.

Effective stride length The amount of stride length behind a walker's body. A racewalker should attempt to maximize stride length behind the body, and limit the length of the stride in front of the body.

Ergogenic aids Legal or illegal substances ingested by an athlete to potentially increase athletic performance.

Fartlek Swedish for "speed play." Workouts where a walker accelerates and decelerates randomly throughout the workout.

Fast-twitch muscle fibers Muscle fibers that produce energy "glycolytically," by breaking down glycogen in the absence of oxygen. They produce rapid contractions, but create lactic acid as a by-product. Some fast-twitch fibers are convertible to non-lactate producing slow-twitch fibers.

Flight phase The short period of the stride where both of a walker's feet are off the ground. A flight phase increases a walker's effective stride length, but slows down stride frequency.

Glycogen Carbohydrate stored in the liver and muscles. Glycogen is used as a fuel during exercise.

Glycolysis The creation of energy through the intra-muscular combustion of glycogen.

Heart rate reserve (HRR) The difference between a walker's resting and maximum heart rates.

Lactic Acid Also referred to as "lactate." Lactic acid is a by-product of anaerobic glycolysis. Although used as a fuel by the heart, excessive lactic acid slows down contractions of the skeletal muscles, preventing you from walking fast.

Lactate threshold The point at which lactate begins to increase in the muscles and blood faster than it can be broken down.

Lactate threshold intervals Near-race pace intervals of 400 meters to 5 kilometers in duration with short rests between each, used to "teach" a walker's muscles to produce energy aerobically, without creating lactic acid as a by-product.

Lifting The failure to maintain contact with the ground at all times while racewalking.

Maximum heart rate (MHR) The highest number of times a walker's heart can beat in a minute of exercising. Maximum heart rate is a genetically determined "random" variable; it has no bearing on a walker's current fitness or potential as an athlete.

Resting heart rate (RHR) The number of times a walker's heart beats per minute while at complete rest. Resting heart rate will decrease as the walker's heart becomes larger and stronger with training. A low resting heart rate is an indicator of fitness.

Single-support phase The part of a racewalker's stride when the straightened leg is directly under the body.

Slow-twitch muscle fibers Muscle fibers that produce energy by converting fats into energy aerobically. They are not able to contract as quickly as fast twitch fibers, but they do not produce lactic acid as a by-product.

Tempo training A type of sustained lactate threshold training that approaches a walker's race pace and race distance. Steady-state tempo workouts are walked at a continuous pace; acceleration tempo workouts are walked at an ever-increasing pace.

Vaulting phase The component of a racewalker's stride where the straightened leg pushes back, vaulting the body forward.

VO$_2$ max A measure of the maximum amount of oxygen that a walker can take in and process during exercise. It is measured in milliliters of oxygen per kilogram of body mass per minute. It is *one* measure of a walker's athletic potential.

VO₂ max intervals *Very* fast 400- to 1,600-meter repeats with long rest intervals between each, used by walkers to increase their ability to take in and process large volumes of oxygen while walking at high speeds.

REFERENCES

Bompa, Tudor. "Peaking for the Major Competitions, Parts I and II," *Science Periodical on Research and Technology in Sport,* April and May, 1984.

Burroughs, Roger and John Fitzgerald. "The Women's 10 Kilometres Race Walk Event," *New Studies in Athletics*, Vol. 5:3, September 1990, pp. 39-44.

Cavagna, Giovanni A., and P. Franzetti. "Mechanics of Competition Walking," *Journal of Applied Physiology*, Vol. 81, 1981, pp. 243-251.

Clippinger-Robertson, Karen. "Abdominal Strength for Race Walkers," unpublished, 1986.

Clippinger-Robertson, Karen. "Flexibility for Race Walkers," unpublished, 1986.

Edwards, Sally. *The Heart Rate Monitor Book,* Polar, CIC, Port Washington, NY, 1994.

Fenker, Richard M. "Imagery Training for Olympic Athletes," unpublished.

Fenton, Mark, and Dave McGovern. *Precision Walking,* Polar Electro, Port Washington, NY, 1995.

Hagburg, James M., and Edward F. Coyle. "Physiological Determinants of Endurance Performance as Studied in Competitive Racewalkers," *Medicine and Science in Sports and Exercise*, Vol. 15, No. 4, pp. 287-289, 1983.

Hausleber, J. "Race Walking Technique," *Track and Field Journal,* Vol. 33, Spring 1987, pp. 5-8.

Hilliard, Craig. "Weight Training and Conditioning for Walkers," *Modern Athlete and Coach*, Vol. 29:2, April 1991, pp. 36-38.

Hopkins, Julian. "Improving Performance in the 50 Kilometres Walk," *New Studies in Athletics*, Vol. 5:3, September 1990, pp. 45-48.

Knicker, Axel and Michael Loch. "Race Walking Technique and Judging—The Final Report of the International Athletic Foundation Research Project," *New Studies in Athletics* Vol. 5:3, September 1990, pp. 25-38.

Lassen, Palle. "The Basic Movement," in *XVI IAAF Race Walking World Cup Official Program,* April, 1993, pp. 22-26.

Marin, Jose. "Controlling the Development of Training in Race Walkers," *New Studies in Athletics*, Vol. 5:3, September 1990, pp. 49-53.

Menier, D.R., and L. G. C. E. Pugh. "The Relation of Oxygen Intake and Velocity of Running in Competition Walkers," *Journal of Physiology*, 1981, Vol. 197, pp. 717-721.

Murray, et al, "Kinematic and Electromyographic Patterns of Olympic Race Walkers," *The American Journal of Sports Medicine*, 1983, Vol. II.

Noakes, Tim, M.D. *Lore of Running,* Leisure Press, Champaign, IL, 1991.

Olan, Ben, ed. *Pursuit of Excellence: The Olympic Story,* The Associated Press and Grolier, Danbury, CT, 1979.

Padilla, Jesús Jiménez, ed. "La Caminata de Competencia," in *METAS de la Juventud y el Deporte,* Special edition, October, 1990.

Palamarchuck, Dr. Howard J., and Dr. Lawrence Kalker. "A Medical Guide for the Race Walker: Information, Recognition, Management and Self-Treatment of Common Injuries and Problems," unpublished.

Payne, A. H. "A Comparison of the Ground Forces in Race Walking With those in Normal Walking and Running," In *Biomechanics, VIA,* Vol. 2A. pp. 293-302. ed. Asmussen. E. and Jorgensen, K. University Park Press, Copenhagen, 1980.

Rudow, Martin. *Advanced Racewalking,* Technique Publications, Seattle, WA, 1987.

Salvage, Jeff and Westerfield, Gary. *Walk Like an Athlete,* Salvage Writes Publications, Marlton, NJ, 1996.

Summers, Harry. "Placement of the Leading Foot in Race Walking," *Modern Athlete and Coach,* Vol. 29:1, January 1991, pp. 33-35.

Trowbridge, E.A. "Walking or Running - When does Lifting Occur?" *Athletics Coach,* 1981, Vol. I, p. 15.

Williams, Idris. "Technical Weekend in the Lake District," *(British) Race Walking Record,* No. 591, January 1992, pp. 11-13.

Yoshida, T., et al. "Physiological Determinants of Race Walking Performance in Female Race Walkers," *British Journal of Sports Medicine,* Vol. 23 (4), pp. 250-254.

Yukelson, Dave and Fenton, Mark. "Psychological Considerations in Race Walking," *Track and Field Quarterly*, Spring 1992, pp. 72-76.

ABOUT THE AUTHOR

Dave McGovern is a member of the U.S. National Racewalk Team and a 14-time National Champion at all distances from 10 to 40 kilometers. His personal-best time of 1:24:29 ranks him as the 5th fastest 20km walker in U.S. history. A USA Track & Field certified coach, Dave is the co-coach of the Mobile chapter of the Leukemia Society of America's marathon Team in Training and the coach of the National Racewalk Teams of Fiji and Ghana. Over the years Dave has taught thousands to racewalk faster and more legally, with fewer injuries, through his "Dave's World Class" week-long training camps and weekend clinics. A writer for *Walking* magazine, Dave is a rare individual: A first-rate coach and athlete, able to communicate his ideas in a witty, easy-to-understand style.